How to Come Out of Your Comfort Zone

Dr Windy Dryden was born in London in 1950. He has worked in psycho-therapy and counselling for over 35 years, and is the author or editor of more than 195 books, including *How to Accept Yourself* (1999), *Coping with Life's Challenges: Moving on from Adversity* (2010), *Coping with Envy* (2010), *How to Develop Inner Strength* (2011), *Coping with Manipulation* (2011) and *Transforming Eight Deadly Emotions into Healthy Ones* (2012), which are published by Sheldon Press.

Overcoming Common Problems Series

Selected titles

A full list of titles is available from Sheldon Press,
36 Causton Street, London SW1P 4ST and on our website at
www.sheldonpress.co.uk

Overcoming Common Problems

How to Come Out of Your Comfort Zone

DR WINDY DRYDEN

First published in Great Britain in 2012

Sheldon Press
36 Causton Street
London SW1P 4ST
www.sheldonpress.co.uk

British Library Cataloguing-in-Publication Data
A catalogue record for this book is available from the British Library

ISBN 978-1-84709-136-9

Typeset by Caroline Waldron, Wirral, Cheshire
First printed in Great Britain by Ashford Colour Press
Subsequently digitally printed in Great Britain

Produced on paper from sustainable forests

Contents

1

What is a comfort zone?

Introduction

In this book, I am going to show you how you can come out and stay out of your comfort zone when it is healthy for you to do so. Traditionally, the term 'comfort zone' means a notional area of comfort which defines a part of your life where you play safe. Thus, when someone says that she (in this case) is afraid to come out of her comfort zone she probably means the following:

1 She is currently in a life-space where she is comfortable, but somewhat unfulfilled.
2 She would like to effect change in this area and do something different and potentially more fulfilling.
3 She is afraid to effect change so she remains within her 'comfort zone'.

People who want to come out of their comfort zone but are afraid to do so often say that they are in a rut. If you are in a rut and afraid to come out of and stay out of this comfort zone, then I will help you to do so. I discuss ruts and how to come out and stay out of them in Chapter 6 and refer throughout this book to the case of Geraldine, who has precisely this problem.

While 'comfort zone' has this precise meaning in the public psyche, I am going to use it more broadly in this book. Specifically, I will discuss two different types of comfort zone situations. In the first, you are in a comfort zone, but you need to come out of it in order to do something that you find difficult or uncomfortable so that you can achieve your goals. However, you don't do so. In this type of comfort zone you experience the following problems:

- procrastination;
- being in a rut;
- lack of persistence.

This type of self-defeating comfort zone is outlined as follows:

Comfort zone → activity that is uncomfortable which will help you to achieve your goals → which you don't do → remain in comfort zone

In the second type of comfort zone, you are in an uncomfortable state which it is in your best interests to tolerate so that you can achieve your goals. However, instead you act to get rid of this discomfort and seek to go into your comfort zone. In this type of comfort zone you experience the following problems:

- difficulty dealing with urges;
- difficulty tolerating unpleasant feelings and thoughts;
- impatience.

This type of self-defeating comfort zone is outlined as follows:

Discomfort (staying with this discomfort will help you to achieve your goals) → you seek comfort (in your comfort zone)

Comfort is not intrinsically problematic

As you will have read, I am only interested in helping you to come out of and stay out of a comfort zone that is unhelpful to you in the longer term. You may be in a comfort zone that is not unhealthy for you and, indeed, you may be in a comfort zone that works for you. That is why when I refer to a comfort zone that is self-defeating for you, I will use the abbreviation 'SDCZ', which stands for 'self-defeating comfort zone'.

Following on from this, let me be quite clear that there is nothing inherently wrong with comfort. Indeed, being comforted by a loving caregiver when you were distressed as a baby or as a child (or even as an adult) is very therapeutic. Such comfort may be expressed verbally or non-verbally (or both) and it helps to soothe and heal.

Also, when you come home having had a hard day at work and you sit down with a refreshing cup of tea in your favourite armchair, listening to some soothing music, then such comfort can have great restorative powers. No, far from viewing comfort as being negative, it can be positive across a lot of situations.

However, as I will show in this book, seeking comfort can also be problematic. Thus, if it is healthy for you to be uncomfortable in the sense that doing so helps you to achieve your goals and you decide to seek comfort instead, then your comfort-seeking is problematic. So seeking comfort is not a problem per se, but if it prevents you from achieving your healthy goals then it is problematic and needs attention.

Let me now provide you with an outline of the chapters that follow. In the next chapter, I am going to outline some of the key ideas that inform this book. These ideas stem from a therapy known as Rational-Emotive Cognitive Behavioural Therapy (RECBT), an approach to counselling and psychotherapy that was originated by Dr Albert Ellis (1913–2007), one of the grandfathers of the therapeutic tradition known as Cognitive Behavioural Therapy (CBT). I will present and discuss the 'ABC' model of RECBT which will help you to understand the factors involved that keep people in general in their SDCZs.

In Chapter 3, I will show you how you can use the 'ABC' model to understand why *you* are in your SDCZ and then set goals to come out of it.

In Chapter 4, I will show you what you need to do to come out and stay out of your SDCZ when it is healthy for you to do so, without experiencing disturbed emotions, behaviour and thinking.

In Chapter 5, I will identify and discuss ten of the major obstacles that you might encounter along the path of coming out of and staying out of your SDCZ, and I will then show you how you can deal with them if you encounter them.

In Chapters 6 and 7, I draw upon the material that I presented in Chapters 2–5 and discuss in general terms the problems that people experience in the two different types of self-defeating comfort zones that I outlined earlier: (a) where you do not move out of your comfort zone in order to engage in activities that you find uncomfortable, but that will help you achieve your goals, and (b) where you get rid of discomfort when it is in your interest to tolerate it in order to achieve your goals.

Finally, in Chapter 8, I provide some advice on how to get the most from this book.

2

The 'ABCs' of Rational-Emotive Cognitive Behavioural Therapy

The approach that I will be taking to help you to come out and stay out of your comfort zone is known as Rational-Emotive Cognitive Behavioural Therapy (RECBT). The term 'Cognitive Behavioural Therapy' (or CBT) defines the therapeutic tradition where it is generally accepted that people's problems are largely determined by the way they think about the adversities that they face in life and how they act in the face of these adversities.

There are quite a few specific approaches within the CBT tradition, and the one on which this book is based is known as 'Rational Emotive Behavioural Therapy', which was established in 1955 by the famous American clinical psychologist Dr Albert Ellis. I call this approach 'Rational-Emotive Cognitive Behavioural Therapy' (RECBT) to show both that it falls within the CBT tradition and that its distinctive features owe a great deal to Dr Ellis.

In this chapter, I will outline the major principles of RECBT that are particularly relevant to helping you understand how people remain within their comfort zone when it is not healthy for them to do so and how they can come out of their comfort zone.

The 'ABCs' of RECBT

RECBT proposes what is known as the 'ABC' model, which is designed to help people understand how they largely create their self-defeating comfort zone (henceforth called SDCZ) and what they need to change to come out of it. I will discuss each element of the 'ABC' model later in this chapter, but let me briefly define each element before we proceed.

A = Activating event (the aspect of the situation that a person is in that she responds to)
B = Beliefs (the beliefs she holds about this activating event)
C = Consequences (the consequences of her beliefs).

People largely create their SDCZ

You may have been surprised to read the words 'largely create' in the previous section. Surely, this is a mistake. Surely nobody would create their own comfort zone if it was unhealthy for them to do so, would they? Actually, they would and they do . . . and you may well do so yourself. The view that people largely create their own SDCZ was put forward many years ago by Epictetus, a leading Stoic philosopher, who argued that events, on their own, do not have the power to disturb people. Rather, it is the way that people think about these events that largely determines whether or not they feel disturbed. This is the basic principle behind the 'ABC' model. Since people are largely responsible for the way they think, it follows that they largely create their SDCZ by the way they think about comfort-related events.

This does not mean that people should blame themselves for largely creating their SDCZ. Far from it! Indeed, if they do blame themselves for largely creating their SDCZ, this is a great way of ensuring that they will stay within this zone! Rather than blaming themselves for creating their SDCZ, it is important that people take responsibility for their creation but do so within a philosophy characterized by self-acceptance and compassion. This philosophy will help people take a cool look at the factors responsible for them staying within their SDCZ, so that they can come out of it. Self-blame will just add to their discomfort and will increase the chances that they will avoid considering these factors. And if people don't understand the factors that are responsible for their being in their SDCZ, they won't know how to get themselves out of it.

Understanding the situation in which a person's 'ABC' occurs

When a person responds to something (what is called an activating event in RECBT), this happens within a specific situation. Here are a few examples:

- Fay was offered a cigarette by a co-worker in her tea-break.
- Brian was in his study at 2 p.m. having promised himself that he would start his essay at that time.
- Harry was standing in a long queue at the supermarket check-out.
- Geraldine was looking at jobs online.

'A' = Activating event

While it is useful to understand the situation that a person is in, it is important to recognize that when a person responds in this situation it is to a particular aspect of this situation, and this aspect needs to be understood. This aspect is known as the 'A' or activating event. When the person is in her SDCZ, it is likely that she is responding to an aspect of the situation that she is in that is negative. Her response to this negative aspect is to seek immediate comfort. Here are some examples of negative 'A's which I will refer to as 'adversities'. In all these examples, in response to the 'A', the person concerned stayed in his or her comfort zone.

- When Fay was offered a cigarette by a co-worker in her tea-break she took it when she experienced a strong urge to smoke. This urge was Fay's 'A'.
- Brian was in his study at 2 p.m., having promised himself that he would start his essay at that time. He didn't start when he thought, 'The essay will be very difficult.' The inference that the essay would be very difficult was Brian's 'A'.
- Harry was standing in a long queue at the supermarket check-out. He lost his temper and left the supermarket when he experienced frustration-related discomfort while waiting. This discomfort was Harry's 'A'.
- Geraldine was looking at jobs online. She did not apply for any when she realized she would lose her familiar – but unfulfilling – routine at her current job. This predicted loss of familiarity was Geraldine's 'A'.

'B' = beliefs

When a person faces an adversity (or negative activating event) at 'A', it is the beliefs that she holds about this adversity that largely determine her response towards it rather than the adversity itself. As we say in RECBT, 'A' does not cause 'C'; rather, 'B' about 'A' largely determines 'C'. This is shown in the equation: 'A' × 'B' → 'C'.

There are two types of beliefs that a person can hold about an adversity. In RECBT terminology these are known as 'irrational' and 'rational' beliefs and I will use these words in this book. However, if you don't resonate with this language you can use the terms 'unhealthy' and 'healthy' or 'unhelpful' and 'helpful', or similar words as you see fit. The important point is that you understand the differences between what I am calling irrational and rational beliefs, a subject to which I will now turn.

Irrational beliefs

There are two types of irrational beliefs. One is known as a rigid belief and it is at the core of an unhealthy response to adversity. There are three extreme beliefs that are derived from this rigid belief. They are known as an awfulizing belief, a discomfort intolerance belief and a depreciation belief. I will discuss these each in turn.

Rigid beliefs   A rigid belief has two components. In the first, the person asserts her preference, and in the second she asserts the idea that she has to have her preference met. As you will see below, often only the second component is used. Thus:

- Fay's 'A' = The urge to smoke.
  Fay's rigid belief at 'B' = 'I must not experience the urge to smoke, and thus I have to get rid of it immediately.'
- Brian's 'A' = The essay will be very difficult.
  Brian's rigid belief at 'B' = 'The essay must be easier.'
- Harry's 'A' = The discomfort of waiting in a queue.
  Harry's rigid belief at 'B' = 'I must not experience this discomfort.'
- Geraldine's 'A' = Loss of familiarity on changing jobs.
  Geraldine's rigid belief at 'B' = 'I have to experience a sense of familiarity.'

Awfulizing beliefs   An awfulizing belief has two components. In the first, the person asserts the badness of not having her demand met and in the second she asserts the idea that it is terrible not having her demand met. As you will see below, often only the second component is used.

Thus:

- Fay's 'A' = The urge to smoke.
  Fay's awfulizing belief at 'B' = 'It is terrible to experience the urge to smoke.'
- Brian's 'A' = The essay will be very difficult.
  Brian's awfulizing belief at 'B' = 'It would be awful if the essay were very difficult.'
- Harry's 'A' = The discomfort of waiting in a queue.
  Harry's awfulizing belief at 'B' = 'It is terrible having to experience discomfort while queuing.'
- Geraldine's 'A' = Loss of familiarity on changing jobs.
  Geraldine's awfulizing belief at 'B' = 'It would be awful to lose this sense of familiarity.'

Discomfort intolerance beliefs A discomfort intolerance belief has two components. In the first, the person asserts the notion that it is a struggle for her to tolerate the discomfort of not having her demand met, and in the second, she asserts the idea that she can't tolerate not having her demand met. As before and as you will see below, often only the second component is used.

Thus:

- Fay's 'A' = The urge to smoke.
  Fay's discomfort intolerance belief at 'B' = 'I can't tolerate having an urge to smoke.'
- Brian's 'A' = The essay will be very difficult.
  Brian's discomfort intolerance belief at 'B' = 'I could not tolerate it if the essay were very difficult.'
- Harry's 'A' = The discomfort of waiting in a queue.
  Harry's discomfort intolerance belief at 'B' = 'I can't stand the discomfort of waiting in a queue.'
- Geraldine's 'A' = Loss of familiarity on changing jobs.
  Geraldine's discomfort intolerance belief at 'B' = 'I can't put up with losing this sense of familiarity if I were to change jobs.'

Depreciation beliefs   A depreciation belief has two components. In the first component the person rates negatively a part of herself, another person or life in general in the context of not having her demand met, and in the second, she rates negatively the whole of herself, another person or life when her demand is not met. As before and as you will again see below, often only the second component is used.

Thus:

- Fay's 'A' = The urge to smoke.
  Fay's depreciation belief at 'B' = 'The world is rotten for allowing me to experience an urge to smoke.'
- Brian's 'A' = The essay will be very difficult.
  Brian's depreciation belief at 'B' = 'My teacher is bad for giving me a very difficult essay to do.'
- Harry's 'A' = The discomfort of waiting in a queue.
  Harry's depreciation belief at 'B' = 'Life is bad for giving me so much discomfort while I wait in the queue.'
- Geraldine's 'A' = Loss of familiarity on changing jobs.
  Geraldine's depreciation belief at 'B' = 'The world is a bad place for giving me a sense of unfamiliarity if I were to change jobs.'

As I will show you later on in this book, when you come to assess your irrational beliefs while you are staying in your SDCZ although it is healthy for you to come out of it, I suggest that you do the following: always identify your rigid belief (unless you have a good reason for not doing so) and the one derivative irrational belief that best fits your experience. Having dealt with irrational beliefs, I will now go on to discuss the four beliefs put forward by RECBT theory as rational alternatives to irrational beliefs.

Rational beliefs

There are two types of rational beliefs. One is known as a flexible belief and it is at the core of a healthy response to adversity. There are three non-extreme beliefs that are derived from this flexible belief. They are known as: a non-awfulizing belief, a discomfort tolerance belief and an acceptance belief. I will discuss each in turn.

Flexible beliefs   A flexible belief has two components. In the first, the person asserts her preference and in the second, she negates the idea that she has to have her preference met.
Thus:

- Fay's 'A' = The urge to smoke.
  Fay's flexible belief at 'B' = 'I would prefer not to experience the urge to smoke, but I don't have to get rid of it immediately.'
- Brian's 'A' = The essay will be very difficult.
  Brian's flexible belief at 'B' = 'I would like the essay to be easier, but it doesn't have to be so.'
- Harry's 'A' = The discomfort of waiting in a queue.
  Harry's flexible belief at 'B' = 'I would prefer not to experience this discomfort, but that does not mean that I must not experience it.'
- Geraldine's 'A' = Loss of familiarity on changing jobs.
  Geraldine's flexible belief at 'B' = 'I would like to experience a sense of familiarity, but I don't have to do so.'

Non-awfulizing beliefs   A non-awfulizing belief has two components. In the first, the person asserts the badness of not having her preference met, and in the second she negates the idea that it is terrible not having her preference met.
Thus:

- Fay's 'A' = The urge to smoke.
  Fay's non-awfulizing belief at 'B' = 'It is bad to experience the urge to smoke, but it is not terrible.'
- Brian's 'A' = The essay will be very difficult.
  Brian's non-awfulizing belief at 'B' = 'It would be bad if the essay were very difficult, but it would not be awful.'
- Harry's 'A' = The discomfort of waiting in a queue.
  Harry's non-awfulizing belief at 'B' = 'It is unfortunate to experience this discomfort, but it is not the end of the world.'
- Geraldine's 'A' = Loss of familiarity on changing jobs.
  Geraldine's non-awfulizing belief at 'B' = 'It would be bad to lose this sense of familiarity, but it would not be awful.'

Discomfort tolerance beliefs   A discomfort tolerance belief has three components. In the first, the person asserts the notion that it is a struggle for her to tolerate the discomfort of not having her preference met, in the second she negates the idea that she can't tolerate not having her preference met, and in the third she asserts the idea that it is worth it to her to tolerate this state of affairs.

Thus:

- Fay's 'A' = The urge to smoke.
  Fay's discomfort tolerance belief at 'B' = 'It is hard to tolerate the urge to smoke, but I can tolerate it and it is worth it to me to do so because I want to give up smoking and be healthy.'
- Brian's 'A' = The essay will be very difficult.
  Brian's discomfort tolerance belief at 'B' = 'It would be hard for me to tolerate it if the essay were very difficult, but I could put up with this and it is worth it to me to do so because I don't want to fall behind in my work.'
- Harry's 'A' = The discomfort of waiting in a queue.
  Harry's discomfort tolerance belief at 'B' = 'It is hard for me to stand this discomfort, but it is not unbearable and it is worth bearing because I want the items that I have selected.'
- Geraldine's 'A' = Loss of familiarity on changing jobs.
  Geraldine's discomfort tolerance belief at 'B' = 'It would be a struggle for me to put up with losing this sense of familiarity, but I can put up with it and it would be worth it for me to do so because I want to further my career.'

Acceptance beliefs   An acceptance belief has three components. In the first component, the person rates negatively a part of herself, another person or life in general in the context of not having her preference met, and in the second she negates the idea that she can rate negatively the whole of herself, another person or life when her preference is not met. In the third component, she asserts the idea that she, the other person or life is far too complex to merit a single negative evaluation and needs to be accepted as fallible (in the first two cases) and ever changing.

Thus:

- Fay's 'A' = The urge to smoke.
  Fay's acceptance belief at 'B' = 'It is bad that I have an urge to smoke, but the world is not rotten for allowing me to experience this urge. Rather, the world is an unrateable place where good, bad and neutral things happen. My urge to smoke is an example of just one bad thing that happens in the world and does not and cannot define the world.'

- Brian's 'A' = The essay will be very difficult.
  Brian's acceptance belief at 'B' = 'My teacher is not bad for giving me a very difficult essay to do. He is a fallible human being who has done what, in my view, is a bad thing.'

- Harry's 'A' = The discomfort of waiting in a queue.
  Harry's acceptance belief at 'B' = 'It is bad that I am uncomfortable while I queue, but that does not prove that life is all bad. Life is too complex to be defined by my discomfort.'

- Geraldine's 'A' = Loss of familiarity on changing jobs.
  Geraldine's acceptance belief at 'B' = 'The world is not a bad place for giving me a sense of unfamiliarity if I were to change jobs. That is just one small aspect of the world, which is a place where many good, bad and neutral things happen.'

I suggested at the end of the section on irrational beliefs that when a person comes to assess the irrational beliefs that largely explain why she stays in her SDCZ when it is healthy for her to come out of it, she identifies her rigid belief and the one derivative irrational belief that best matches her experience. When the person comes to develop rational alternatives to these beliefs, it follows that she specify the flexible alternative to her rigid belief and the appropriate alternative to the other derivative irrational belief she identified.

'C' = Consequences of beliefs

When a person holds a set of irrational beliefs about discomfort-related adversities, she tends to remain in her SDCZ. If she were to come out of it while holding such beliefs, she would experience unhealthy negative emotions about the adversities, her behaviour would tend to be unconstructive and her thinking would tend to be highly distorted and skewed to the negative.

When the person holds a set of rational beliefs about discomfort-related adversities, she tends to come out of her SDCZ. And, once out, she tends to stay out as long as she continues those rational beliefs. In doing so, she will experience healthy negative emotions about the adversities, her behaviour will tend to be constructive and her thinking will tend to be realistic and balanced.

I will demonstrate the impact of beliefs at 'B' on emotions, behaviours and subsequent thinking with reference to the examples of Fay, Brian, Harry and Geraldine. In doing so, I will present the person's rigid belief and one other chosen derivative irrational belief and their rational alternatives. When presenting the person's irrational belief, I will demonstrate two different sets of consequences: the first is where the person's irrational beliefs have led him or her to enter or remain in an SDCZ, and the other details how that person would have felt, acted and thought had he or she refrained from entering the SDCZ, or come out of it if he or she was already there, while holding the same irrational beliefs.

Fay

In the first 'ABC', Fay held a set of irrational beliefs. You will see that there are two 'Cs', one where Fay remains in her SDCZ and the other indicating how she would have responded were she to stay out of it.

The impact of Fay's irrational beliefs:

- Situation = I was offered a cigarette by a co-worker in my tea-break.
- 'A' = Experiencing a strong urge to smoke.
- 'B' (rigid belief) = 'I must not experience the urge to smoke, and thus I have to get rid of it immediately.'

  (discomfort intolerance belief) = 'I can't tolerate having an urge to smoke.'
- 'C' (going to the SDCZ)

  (emotion) = None.

  (behaviour) = Taking and smoking the cigarette.

  (thinking) = None.

- 'C' (staying out of the SDCZ)

  (emotion) = Anxiety.

  (behaviour) = Not smoking, getting agitated and then eating chocolate to get rid of the urge to smoke.

  (thinking) = 'I'll go mad if I don't get rid of the urge to smoke.'

This shows that when Fay holds an irrational belief, going back to her SDCZ spares her a lot of emotional pain, behavioural and thinking disturbance that she would experience if she refrained from entering her SDCZ still holding these irrational beliefs. Also, in the latter situation she exchanges one behavioural problem (i.e. smoking) for another (i.e. eating). This helps to explain why a lot of people gain weight when they stop smoking. In short, faced with the choice of going to her SDCZ with her irrational beliefs or refraining from entering her SDCZ with those same irrational beliefs, Fay's decision to stay in her SDCZ appears to be the lesser of the two evils.

However, as I will now show you, Fay has a third option, to stay out of her SDCZ while holding a set of rational beliefs. Let me spell out the difference these rational beliefs would have made to Fay.

The impact of Fay's rational beliefs:

- Situation = I was offered a cigarette by a co-worker in my tea-break.
- 'A' = Experiencing a strong urge to smoke.
- 'B' (flexible belief) = 'I would prefer not to experience the urge to smoke, but that does not mean that I must not experience it or get rid of it immediately.'

  (discomfort tolerance belief) = 'It is hard to tolerate the urge to smoke, but I can tolerate it and it is worth it to me to do so, because I want to give up smoking and be healthy.'
- 'C' (emotion) = Concern.

  (behaviour) = Not smoking, feeling uncomfortable, but not doing anything to get rid of the urge to smoke. Going back to work at the end of the tea-break.

  (thinking) = 'The urge to smoke will reduce in intensity and go away after a while.'

As you can see, Fay's rational beliefs helped her to stay out of her SDCZ and deal with the discomfort of not smoking a cigarette when she felt the urge to do so.

Brian

In the first 'ABC', Brian held a set of irrational beliefs.
You will see that there are two 'Cs', one where Brian remains in his SDCZ and the other indicating how he would have responded were he to come out of it.

The impact of Brian's irrational beliefs:

- Situation = I was in my study at 2 p.m. having promised myself that I would start my essay at that time.
- 'A' = The essay will be very difficult.
- 'B' (rigid belief) = 'The essay must be easier.'

  (awfulizing belief) = 'It would be awful if the essay were very difficult.'
- 'C' (going to the SDCZ)

  (emotion) = Uneasy but not anxious.

  (behaviour) = Puts off working on the essay.

  (thinking) = 'I'll do it later when I am in a better frame of mind.'
- 'C' (staying out of the SDCZ)

  (emotion) = Anxiety.

  (behaviour) = Pacing up and down, engaging in distracting activities, but anxiously.

  (thinking) = 'I'll never finish this essay'; 'I'll fail the course.'

This analysis shows that when Brian holds an irrational belief, going back to his SDCZ spares him a lot of emotional pain, behavioural and thinking disturbance that he would experience if he came out of his SDCZ still holding these irrational beliefs. However, note that he is still feeling uneasy in his SDCZ, and even though he uses rationalization thinking here his uneasiness indicates that he has not completely fooled himself. In short, faced with the choice of remaining in his SDCZ with his irrational beliefs or coming out of his SDCZ with those same irrational beliefs, Brian's choice to stay in his SDCZ again appears to be the lesser of the two evils for him.

However, as I will now show you, Brian has a third option: to come out of his SDCZ while holding a set of rational beliefs. Let me spell out the difference these rational beliefs would have made for Brian.

The impact of Brian's rational beliefs:

- Situation = I was in my study at 2 p.m. having promised myself that I would start my essay at that time.

- 'A' = The essay will be very difficult.
- 'B' (flexible belief) = 'I would like the essay to be easier, but it doesn't have to be so.'

  (non-awfulizing belief) = 'It would be bad if the essay were very difficult, but it would not be awful.'
- 'C' (emotion) = Concern.

  (behaviour) = Starting work on the essay even though uncomfortable.

  (thinking) = 'It may be very difficult and I may need help, but if I persist I will probably finish it'; 'If I work hard and do essays like this one, I will probably pass the course.'

As you can see, Brian's rational beliefs helped him to come out of his SDCZ and deal with the discomfort of starting an essay that he thought would be very difficult. In the event, once Brian got into the essay he discovered that it was easier than he thought it would be. This is typical of people who procrastinate: they routinely overestimate the difficulty of a task and find once they have got into it that it is not as difficult as predicted.

Harry

In the first 'ABC', Harry held a set of irrational beliefs. You will again see that there are two 'Cs', one where Harry goes into his SDCZ and the other indicating how he would have responded were he to stay out of it.

The impact of Harry's irrational beliefs:

- Situation = I was standing in a long queue at the supermarket check-out.
- 'A' = The discomfort of waiting in the queue.
- 'B' (rigid belief) = 'I must not experience this discomfort.'

  (discomfort intolerance belief) = 'I can't stand the discomfort of waiting in a queue.'
- 'C' (SDCZ response)

  (emotion) = Relieved but still an underlying sense of anger.

  (behaviour) = Angrily leaving the queue.

  (thinking) = 'I am not going to give this lousy supermarket my business.'
- 'C' (staying out of the SDCZ)

  (emotion) = Unhealthy anger.

(behaviour) = Staying in the queue, but increasingly acting in an angry, agitated manner (e.g. swearing and aggressively calling to see the manager).

(thinking) = 'If this queue doesn't move more quickly I'll explode.'

This analysis shows that when Harry holds an irrational belief, going back to his SDCZ spares him a lot of emotional pain and behavioural and thinking disturbance that he would experience if he came out of his SDCZ still holding these irrational beliefs. However, note that he is still feeling an underlying sense of anger in his SDCZ, although he is not nearly as angry as he would have been if he had come out of his SDCZ by remaining in the queue. Thus, faced with the choice of going to his SDCZ with his irrational beliefs or remaining out of his SDCZ with those same irrational beliefs, Harry's choice to go to his SDCZ appears to be the lesser of the two evils for him.

However, as with Fay and Brian, Harry has a third option, to come out of his SDCZ while holding a set of rational beliefs. Let me spell out the difference these rational beliefs would have made for Harry.

The impact of Harry's rational beliefs:

- Situation = I was standing in a long queue at the supermarket check-out.
- 'A' = The discomfort of waiting in a queue.
- 'B' (flexible belief) = 'I would prefer not to experience this discomfort, but that does not mean that I must not experience it.'

  (discomfort tolerance belief) = 'It is hard for me to stand this discomfort, but it is not unbearable and it is worth bearing because I want the items that I have selected.'
- 'C' (emotion) = Healthy anger.

  (behaviour) = Staying in the queue but concentrating on writing emails on my phone or doing a Sudoku puzzle.

  (thinking) = 'I am not going to explode. Rather, I am going to have a polite word with the manager to open up more check-outs when I get out of this queue.'

As you can see, Harry's rational beliefs helped him to stay out of his SDCZ and deal with the discomfort of waiting in a supermarket queue.

Geraldine

In the first 'ABC', Geraldine held a set of irrational beliefs. You will again see that there are two 'Cs', one where Geraldine remains in her SDCZ and the other indicating how she would have responded were she to come out of it.

The impact of Geraldine's irrational beliefs:

- Situation = I was looking at jobs online.
- 'A' = The loss of familiarity I would experience if I were to get a more challenging job.
- 'B' (rigid belief) = 'I have to experience a sense of familiarity.'

  (discomfort intolerance belief) = 'I would not be able to put up with losing this sense of familiarity if I were to change jobs.'
- 'C' (staying in the SDCZ)

  (emotion) = Relieved but with a sense of unfulfilment.

  (behaviour) = Deciding not to apply for any jobs that I really want.

  (thinking) = 'The time is not right for me to apply for another job.'
- 'C' = (coming out of the SDCZ)

  (emotion) = Anxiety.

  (behaviour) = Playing safe by only applying online for a slightly better job that would involve the minimum upheaval, but not applying for jobs I really want which would involve much greater challenge and upheaval.

  (thinking) = 'I want a new, challenging and fulfilling job, but I will never be able to settle at it.'

Once again, this analysis shows that when Geraldine holds an irrational belief, staying in her SDCZ spares her from feeling anxious and from having highly negative thoughts that she would experience if she came out of her SDCZ still holding these irrational beliefs. However, note that she is still unfulfilled in her SDCZ. Thus, yet again, faced with the choice of remaining in her SDCZ with her irrational beliefs or coming out of her SDCZ with those same irrational beliefs, Geraldine's choice to stay in her SDCZ appears to be the lesser of the two evils for her.

However, as with Fay, Brian and Harry, Geraldine has a third option, to come out of her SDCZ while holding a set of rational beliefs. Let me spell out the difference these rational beliefs would have made for Geraldine.

The impact of Geraldine's rational beliefs:

- Situation = I was looking at jobs online.
- 'A' = The loss of familiarity I would experience if I were to get a challenging job.
- 'B' (flexible belief) = 'I would like to experience a sense of familiarity, but I don't have to do so.'

  (discomfort tolerance belief) = 'It would be a struggle for me to put up with losing this sense of familiarity, but I can put up with it and it would be worth it for me to do so because I want to further my career.'
- 'C' (emotion) = Concern.

  (behaviour) = Applying for three new jobs online that I really want.

  (thinking) = 'It will be difficult for me to settle at a new, challenging job, but I will be able to do so eventually.'

As you can see, Geraldine's rational beliefs would help her to come out of her SDCZ and deal with the discomfort of leaving a familiar but unfulfilling job and settling into a new, unfamiliar, challenging job.

In the next chapter, I will show you how you can use the 'ABC' model to help you understand why you are in *your* self-defeating comfort zone and the importance of setting goals to come out and stay out of it.

3

Understanding why you are in your self-defeating comfort zone and setting goals to come out and stay out of it

Introduction

In the last chapter, I introduced you to the 'ABC' model of RECBT. This model is designed to help people to understand why they are in a self-defeating comfort zone (SDCZ). In particular, this model shows that a key ingredient to whether you stay in or come out of your SDCZ is the beliefs that you hold about the specific form of discomfort related to this zone. In addition, I discussed the cases of Fay, Brian, Harry and Geraldine and detailed the irrational beliefs that kept them in their particular SDCZ and the rational alternative beliefs that they would have to hold if they were to come out of and stay out of their SDCZ.

In this chapter, I am going to show you how you can use the 'ABC' model to understand why you are in your SDCZ and then set goals to come out of it. In Chapter 2, I presented the 'ABC' model in alphabetical order. When it comes to assessing your SDCZ and setting goals to come out of it, I suggest that you use the order 'CAB' when you assess the factors that are relevant to why you are in your SDCZ, since identifying how you feel, act and think (at 'C') in response to an adversity will often assist you in identifying the often elusive nature of 'A'. However, you may assess 'A' before 'C' if you want to. Once you have assessed 'A' and 'C' (in whatever order you have chosen to do that), you can then assess 'B'.

In Chapter 1, I discussed how you can tell if you are in an SDCZ and I suggest that you review that material if you need to. In this chapter, I will assume that you have decided that you are in an SDCZ and that you want to come out of it. So here are the steps that I recommend you to take.

Step 1: Describe your SDCZ and why it is a problem for you

The very first step in any self-help programme should be specifying your problem and why it is a problem for you. Let me illustrate how Fay, Brian, Harry and Geraldine did this.

- *Fay's problem*
  My self-defeating comfort zone (SDCZ) is smoking cigarettes. Whenever I feel the urge to smoke, I do so. This is a problem for me because I am jeopardizing my health.

- *Brian's problem*
  My SDCZ is procrastination. Whenever I anticipate starting things that are in my interest to do, I put off doing them. This is a problem for me because I am always chasing my tail and can never relax even when I am procrastinating.

- *Harry's problem*
  My SDCZ is angry impatience. Whenever I have to wait, I get angry and leave the situation when it is in my interest to stay. This is a problem for me in that I end up wasting time by going to places at inconvenient times to avoid the queues.

- *Geraldine's problem*
  My SDCZ is that I am in a rut at work. Whenever I promise myself that I will look for a new, more challenging job, I don't follow through with it and stay with my present job.

Now it's your turn to describe your SDCZ and to specify how this is a problem for you. Take a piece of paper or a notebook and jot down the answers to these two questions:

- What is my SDCZ?
- What are the reasons that this is a problem for me?

Step 2: Identify your goal and the reasons why you want to achieve it

In any self-change programme, it is important that you understand what you are aiming for. It is not sufficient for you to say:

'I recognize that I am in a self-defeating comfort zone and I want to come out of it.' You also need to specify what you would be doing, feeling and/or thinking differently if you were out of your SDCZ. In short, you need to specify your goal and why you want to achieve it. Here is how Fay, Brian, Harry and Geraldine specified their problems and goals.

- *Fay's goal*
  I want to come out and stay out of my comfort zone by stopping smoking because it will be much better for my health.
- *Brian's goal*
  I want to start tasks that are in my interest to do, rather than put them off.
- *Harry's goal*
  Whenever I have to wait, I want to stay in the situation when it is in my interest to do so.
- *Geraldine's goal*
  Whenever I promise myself that I will look for a new, more challenging job, I want to follow through with it and apply for such positions until I obtain one.

Now it's your turn to specify your goal with respect to coming out of your SDCZ. In your notebook, answer these questions:

- If I came out and stayed out of my SDCZ, in what ways would I change?
- Why is this important to me?

Once you have described the problem and set goals, the next step is to assess the problem. There are two ways of doing this. The first approach is to assess a typical and specific example of you going to your SDCZ. Here you are assessing what actually happened. The second approach is to assess what you would have experienced if you had not gone to your SDCZ. I will discuss both.

Step 3a: Assess your SDCZ using the 'ABC' model – consider what actually happened

In this step, I am going to show you how to assess a typical example of when you went to your SDCZ, using the 'ABC' model. As you will see, there are inherent problems in taking this approach, but it is possible to do it this way. As I have said, when I have shown you how to assess what actually happened, I will present an alternative approach to assessment which focuses on what you would have experienced if you had not gone to your SDCZ.

I recommended earlier in this chapter that you use the 'ABC' framework to assess your SDCZ in the order 'CAB' (although you can also use the order 'ACB'). When you use this model, I suggest that you use a typical example of your SDCZ. Doing so will help you to get the specific information that you need to assess the problem.

Describe the situation you were in

It is often useful for you to describe the situation you were in when you went to your SDCZ. As you do so, make sure that your description is just that – a description. Exclude any interpretations or inferences. Here are the situations described by Fay, Brian, Harry and Geraldine.

- Fay was offered a cigarette by a co-worker in her tea-break.
- Brian was in his study at 2 p.m. having promised himself that he would start his essay at that time.
- Harry was standing in a long queue at the supermarket check-out.
- Geraldine was looking at jobs online.

Now it is your turn to describe the situation you were in when you went to your SDCZ. In your notebook, describe the situation you were in when you went to your SDCZ.

Having described the situation in which you went to your SDCZ, you are now ready to assess 'C'.

Assess 'C'

As I pointed out in Chapter 2, there are three components of 'C': emotional, behavioural and thinking. However, I will discuss them in the order behavioural, emotional and thinking, for reasons that will soon become apparent.

Assess the behavioural 'C'

Perhaps the most obvious sign that you are in a SDCZ is that you are acting in ways that are designed to avoid or eliminate (a) the kind of discomfort that you find particularly difficult to deal with, and (b) the associated emotions and thinking that would accompany such discomfort if you allowed yourself to experience it.

Here are questions Fay, Brian, Harry and Geraldine asked themselves to identify their behavioural 'Cs'.

Fay:
- Question: What did I do when I was offered a cigarette by my co-worker in the tea-break to go to my SDCZ?
- Answer: I took the cigarette and smoked it.

Brian:
- Question: What did I do at 2 p.m. to go to my SDCZ?
- Answer: I put off working on my essay rather than starting it.

Harry:
- Question: What did I do while I was standing in a long queue at the supermarket check-out to go to my SDCZ?
- Answer: I angrily left the queue.

Geraldine:
- Question: What did I do when I was looking at jobs online to go to my SDCZ?
- Answer: I did not apply for jobs that I would love to have.

Now it is your turn to identify your behaviour when you went to your SDCZ in the situation that you have described. In your notebook, list what you did to go to your SDCZ when you were in the situation that you have described.

Assess the emotional 'C'

One of the major features of being in an SDCZ is that you ward off negative emotions, so that, while you don't experience unhealthy negative emotions, you also don't experience healthy negative emotions either. After a while, you come to think that all negative feelings must be avoided.

What follows from this is that identifying emotional 'Cs' in assessing episodes when you went to your SDCZ is problematic. Thus, only Harry could have answered the question: 'How did you feel in the situation that you were in?' Harry knew that he felt underlyingly angry just before leaving the queue, but could not tell if his anger was healthy or unhealthy because his behaviour quickly led him away from the situation in which he felt angry, an emotion which was rapidly replaced with relief. Fay, Brian and Geraldine all went to their respective SDCZs before they experienced any distinct negative emotion that they could focus on. Fay could not access any emotions at all, Brian felt uneasy but not anxious, while Geraldine noted that she was relieved, but had an underlying sense of being unfulfilled. Remember that the purpose of behavioural 'Cs' here is to encourage people to go to their SDCZs where they do not experience any sustained negative emotion.

See if you can identify your emotional 'C' by answering the following question in your notebook: when you were in the situation you have described, what emotion did you experience just before you went to your SDCZ?

Don't worry if you can't identify the emotion; three out of four of the people we are following could not do so either.

Assess the thinking 'C'

Going to your SDCZ also means that you tend not to experience the distorted thoughts that you would have if you remained in the situation and did not go to your SDCZ. Your thinking is more likely to justify your behaviour, as we shall see.

When they asked themselves how they thought in the situation that they were in that accompanied their feelings and behaviour, this is what Fay, Brian, Harry and Geraldine said:

- Fay: 'I wasn't thinking anything when I took the cigarette.'
- Brian: 'I'll do it later when I am in a better frame of mind.'
- Harry: 'I am not going to give this lousy supermarket my business.'
- Geraldine: 'The time is not right for me to apply for another job.'

As you can see from these responses, most of our four people justify their behaviour, the purpose of which was to encourage them to go to their SDCZ. If they had stayed in the situation, their thinking would have been much more distorted and, ironically, more helpful in identifying their irrational beliefs.

See if you can identify your thinking 'C' by answering the following question in your notebook:

- When you were in the situation that you have described, what thoughts were going through your mind as you went to your SDCZ?

If you can only identify thinking that justified your behaviour, you are in good company.

In conclusion, when you come to assess your responses to adversity on going to your SDCZ, it is relatively easy to identify your behaviour but it may be more difficult to identify your accompanying emotions and thinking. As I have already explained, the reason for this is that one of the purposes of your SDCZ-seeking behaviour is to protect you from disturbing emotions and thoughts. Thus, when coming to assess your 'A' in your selected example, you can only really rely on behaviour in doing so, as I will now discuss.

Assess 'A'

If you recall from Chapter 2, 'A' is the aspect of the situation you were in that you were disturbed about or, more accurately, you would have been disturbed about if you had kept out of your SDCZ. However, since you did go to your SDCZ, you can assess your 'A' by using your behavioural 'C'. I will demonstrate this by referring to the cases of Fay, Brian, Harry and Geraldine, who asked themselves the following questions:

Fay:
- Question: When I was offered a cigarette, what was I reacting to when I took it?
- Answer: The urge to smoke the cigarette. (This was Fay's 'A'.)

Brian:
- Question: When I was in my study at 2 p.m. having promised myself that I would start my essay at that time, what was I reacting to when I decided not to start it?
- Answer: The thought that the essay would be very difficult. (This was Brian's 'A'.)

Harry:
- Question: When I was standing in a long queue at the supermarket check-out, what was I reacting to when I angrily left the queue?
- Answer: The discomfort of waiting in the queue. (This was Harry's 'A'.)

Geraldine:
- Question: When I was looking at jobs online, what was I reacting to when I decided not to apply for jobs that I would really like?
- Answer: The loss of familiarity that I thought I would experience if I were to change jobs. (This was Geraldine's 'A'.)

See if you can identify your 'A' by answering the following question in your notebook:

- What was I reacting to in the situation I was in when I went to my SDCZ?

Assess 'B'

It is important that you remember at this point that RECBT is based on an 'ABC' model of human functioning and not an 'AC' model, even when 'As' are clearly inferences (that is, hunches about reality that may be correct or incorrect). Thus, it would be tempting for Brian, for example, to conclude that his thought (or inference) 'This essay will be very difficult' caused him not to work on the essay, but this would be incorrect, since it would posit that it was the inferred difficulty of the essay that explains why Brian did not work on it (the 'AC' explanation). If this were true, then it would mean that Brian could only work on the essay if he were sure that it would not be very difficult.

The 'ABC' model, on the other hand, allows Brian to work on the essay even if it were difficult, assuming that Brian holds a set of rational beliefs that allows him to do this. Thus, it is not the difficulty of the essay that explains why Brian did not start work on it, but rather it is the set of irrational beliefs he held about this difficulty that explains his procrastination. This is the 'ABC' model and means that once you have identified the 'C' and 'A' aspects of your entry into your SDCZ, you need to identify the irrational beliefs that are largely responsible for you going to that zone when it is not healthy for you to do so.

Assess your rigid belief

As I outlined in Chapter 2, when you go to your comfort zone when it is not healthy for you to do so, you hold a rigid belief and one or more extreme beliefs that are derived from this rigid belief. I suggest, as a matter of course, that you assess at 'B' your rigid belief and the one extreme belief about 'A' that best accounts for you going to your SDCZ. Start with assessing your rigid belief about your 'A' as did Fay, Brian, Harry and Geraldine. They asked themselves and answered the following questions:

Fay:
• Question: What was I demanding ('B') about my urge to smoke ('A') that led me to smoke ('C')?
• Answer: 'I must not experience the urge to smoke, and thus I have to get rid of it immediately.'

Brian:
• Question: What was I demanding ('B') about the essay being very difficult ('A') that led me to put off starting to work on it ('C')?
• Answer: 'The essay must be easier.'

Harry:
- Question: What was I demanding ('B') about the discomfort of waiting in the supermarket queue ('A') that led me to angrily leave the queue ('C')?
- Answer: 'I must not experience this discomfort.'

Geraldine:
- Question: What was I demanding ('B') about losing the familiarity of changing jobs ('A') that led me not to apply for jobs that I would like to have ('C')?
- Answer: 'I have to have a sense of familiarity.'

See if you can identify your rigid belief at 'B' by answering the following question in your notebook:

- What was I demanding about my 'A' that led me to go to my SDCZ at 'C'?

Assess your most pertinent extreme belief

As I first discussed in Chapter 2, when you hold a rigid belief you also tend to hold one or more extreme beliefs that lead you to go to your SDCZ when it is not healthy for you to do so. There are three such extreme beliefs (awfulizing beliefs, discomfort intolerance beliefs and depreciation beliefs). After you have identified your rigid belief, I suggest that you select the one extreme belief that is most pertinent to you going to your SDCZ. This is what Fay, Brian, Harry and Geraldine did, as shown below.

Fay:
- Question: Which extreme belief best fits my experience of giving in to my urge to smoke?
- Answer: Discomfort intolerance belief: 'I can't tolerate having an urge to smoke.'

Brian:
- Question: Which extreme belief best fits my experience of not starting work on my essay when I thought that it would be very difficult?

- Answer: Awfulizing belief: 'It would be awful if the essay were very difficult.'

Harry:
- Question: Which extreme belief best fits my experience of angrily leaving the supermarket queue because of the discomfort I felt?
- Answer: Discomfort intolerance belief: 'I can't stand the discomfort of waiting in a queue.'

Geraldine:
- Question: Which extreme belief best fits my experience of not applying for jobs that I really wanted when I thought of the unfamiliarity I would have if I changed jobs?
- Answer: Discomfort intolerance belief: 'I would not be able to put up with losing this sense of familiarity if I were to change jobs.'

Now it is your turn to identify your most pertinent extreme belief. In your notebook, answer the following question:

- Which extreme belief best fits my experience of going to my SDCZ when it was not healthy for me to do so?

Step 3b: Assess your SDCZ using the 'ABC' model – consider what would have happened if you had stayed out of your SDCZ

In this alternative approach, I am going to show you how to use the 'ABC' model to assess a typical example of when you felt like going to your SDCZ but didn't do so. This, of course, did not happen, but I want you to imagine that it did. In this way you can deal with issues that you are running away from, as will soon become clear. In short, this alternative approach to assessment focuses on what you would have experienced if you had stayed out of your SDCZ.

I recommended earlier in this chapter that you use the 'ABC' framework to assess a specific example of what happened when you went to your SDCZ, and that you do so in the order 'CAB' (although you can also use the order 'ACB'). When you use this model to assess what you would have experienced if you had stayed out of your SDCZ, use the same specific example and in the same 'CAB' order (although again you can also use the 'ACB' order). The important thing to focus on in this second approach to assessment is that you imagine that you did not go to your SDCZ. If you do this, it will help you to get the specific information that was difficult to assess when you actually went to your SDCZ.

Describe the situation you were in

Describe the situation you were in when you went to your self-defeating comfort zone, but this time imagine that you did not go there. Again, exclude any interpretations or inferences. This should yield the same information as when you described the situation that you were in when you employed the first approach to assessment. Here is a reminder of the situations described by Fay, Brian, Harry and Geraldine.

- Fay was offered a cigarette by a co-worker in her tea-break.
- Brian was in his study at 2 p.m. having promised himself that he would start his essay at that time.
- Harry was standing in a long queue at the supermarket check-out.
- Geraldine was looking at jobs online.

Now it is your turn to describe the situation you were in when you went to your SDCZ. Jot it down in your notebook.

Assess 'C'

Having described the situation you were in when you went to your SDCZ, you are now ready to assess 'C'. This involves identifying how you would have felt, acted and thought if you had stayed out of your SDCZ.

Assess the emotional 'C'

In Chapter 2, I specified how each of the four people we have been following in this book imagined they would respond if they had stayed out of their SDCZ while holding irrational beliefs. Doing this helped them to identify their unhealthy negative emotion at 'C'. Here are the questions that our four people asked themselves to identify their emotional 'C' when employing the second approach to assessment:

Fay:
- Question: How would I have felt if I did not take the cigarette that my co-worker offered me?
- Answer: Anxious.

Brian:
- Question: How would I have felt if I started the essay rather than put it off?
- Answer: Anxious.

Harry:
- Question: How would I have felt if I had stayed in the queue rather than leaving it?
- Answer: Unhealthily angry.

Geraldine:
- Question: How would I have felt if I had applied for challenging jobs online?
- Answer: Anxious.

Now it's your turn to specify your emotional 'C' goal with respect to staying out of your SDCZ. In your notebook, answer the following question:

- If I had stayed out of my SDCZ, what emotion would I have experienced?

Assess the behavioural 'C'

When you assess a typical episode where you went to your SDCZ, then it is fairly easy to identify your behaviour. It is either something that you did or something that you did not do to rid yourself of actual or anticipated discomfort. Thus, Fay took the cigarette, Brian did not start work on his essay, Harry left the supermarket queue and Geraldine did not apply for jobs she really wanted.

In this alternative approach to assessment, you are asked to imagine that you stayed out of your SDCZ and to predict how you would have acted instead. Here is how our four people identified their behavioural 'C' once they imagined themselves staying out of their SDCZ.

Fay:
- Question: What would I have done if I had not taken the cigarette to deal with the urge to smoke?
- Answer: I would have become agitated and then eaten chocolate to get rid of the urge to smoke.

Brian:
- Question: What would I have done if I had not put off working on my essay that I inferred would be very difficult?
- Answer: I would have paced up and down and engaged in distracting activities, but anxiously so.

Harry:
- Question: What would I have done if I had stayed in the queue and faced the discomfort of doing so?
- Answer: I would have acted in an increasingly angry and agitated manner, like swearing and aggressively calling to see the manager.

Geraldine:
- Question: What would I have done if I had not put off applying for jobs online?
- Answer: I would have played safe by only applying for a slightly better job which would have involved the minimum upheaval. I would not have applied for jobs that I really wanted which would have involved much greater challenge and upheaval.

Now it's your turn to identify how you would have behaved if you had stayed out of your comfort zone. In your notebook, answer the following question:

- If I had stayed out of my SDCZ, in what way(s) would I have acted?

Assess the thinking 'C'

When you assess a typical episode where you went to your SDCZ, it is difficult to identify your accompanying thinking since your SDCZ-seeking behaviour is designed to spare you from such distorted thinking. As I discussed earlier in this chapter, only Harry could, with any clarity, identify the thinking that accompanied his SDCZ-seeking behaviour. When you assess the same episode from the perspective of what you would have thought if you had stayed out of your SDCZ, then it becomes easier to identify such thinking, which, as we will see, is likely to be quite distorted and skewed to the negative.

Thus, in this alternative approach to assessment, you are asked to imagine that you stayed out of your SDCZ and to predict how you would have thought instead. Here is how our four people identified their thinking 'C' once they imagined themselves staying out of their SDCZ.

Fay:
- Question: What would I have thought if I had not taken the cigarette to deal with the urge to smoke?
- Answer: 'I'll go mad if I don't get rid of the urge to smoke.'

Brian:
- Question: What would I have thought if I had not put off working on my essay that I inferred would be very difficult?
- Answer: 'I'll never finish this essay, I'll fail the course.'

Harry:
- Question: What would I have thought if I had stayed in the queue and faced the discomfort of doing so?
- Answer: 'If this queue doesn't move more quickly, I'll explode.'

Geraldine:
- Question: What would I have thought if I had not put off applying for jobs online?
- Answer: 'I want a new challenging and fulfilling job, but I will never be able to settle at it.'

Now it's your turn to identify how you would have thought if you had stayed out of your comfort zone. Answer the following question in your notebook:

- If I had stayed out of my SDCZ, what thoughts would I have had?

Assess 'A'

You will remember that 'A' stands for the aspect of the situation that you are responding to which results in you going to your SDCZ. Remember, though, that in this second approach to assessment I have asked you to examine what you would have experienced if you had stayed out of this zone. I have done so because it makes identifying 'C' that much easier. You will have noticed that when you imagine staying out of your SDCZ your emotional, behavioural and thinking 'Cs' show that you are in a disturbed state of mind. If you are going to learn to stay out of your SDCZ, you need to deal with this disturbance.

You can use these 'Cs', particularly the emotional 'C', to identify what you are most disturbed about in the situation which you endeavour to escape from by retreating to your SDCZ. This aspect is 'A'. Here is how Fay, Brian, Harry and Geraldine identified their 'A'.

Fay:
- Question: When my co-worker offered me a cigarette what was I most anxious about?
- Answer: Experiencing the urge to smoke and not smoking.

Brian:
- Question: What was I anxious about with respect to starting the essay?
- Answer: It would be very difficult.

Harry:
- Question: What was I most angry about with respect to waiting in the supermarket queue?
- Answer: The discomfort of waiting in the queue.

Geraldine:

- Question: What was I most anxious about when I was looking online for jobs?
- Answer: The loss of familiarity that I would experience if I were to get a more challenging job.

Now it's your turn to identify your 'A'. In your notebook, answer the following question:

- What was I most [add the unhealthy negative emotion at 'C'] about with respect to the situation I was in?

If you are still having difficulty identifying your 'A', you can use my 'magic question' technique. Here, first, is how Fay used it:

- Question: When my co-worker offered me a cigarette, what one thing would have to happen for me not to feel anxious about this?
- Answer: Not having an urge to smoke.

Thus, the opposite ('having the urge to smoke') is Fay's 'A'.

Here is how you can employ this technique. In your notebook, answer the following question:

- When I was in the situation that I have described, what one thing would have eliminated or significantly reduced my feelings of [add the unhealthy negative emotion at 'C']?

The opposite of this is your 'A'. Write it in your notebook.

Assess 'B'

I have pointed out throughout this book that RECBT is based on an 'ABC' model of human functioning and not an 'AC' model. So even when Fay faces an urge to smoke it is not this 'A' that leads her to smoke, but the beliefs that she holds at 'B' about this urge that are largely responsible for her responses. It follows from this that if she wants to desist from smoking, stay out of her SDCZ and not be disturbed, she needs to develop a different set of beliefs about 'A'.

In this section, I will show you how to identify the irrational beliefs that largely account for the disturbed responses (at 'C') that you thought you would have made to your adversity (at 'A') once you imagined that you had stayed out of your SDCZ.* As I have shown in Chapter 2, an irrational belief can be rigid and extreme. In RECBT, your rigid belief is deemed to be your primary irrational belief and three types of extreme beliefs (i.e. awfulizing beliefs, discomfort intolerance beliefs and depreciation beliefs) are deemed to be derived from this primary rigid belief and are regarded as secondary irrational beliefs. My suggestion is that as a matter of course you identify your rigid belief (since it is primary) and the one extreme belief that best explains your responses at 'C'.

Assess your rigid belief

This is how Fay, Brian, Harry and Geraldine identified their rigid belief.

Fay:
- Question: What was I demanding ('B') about my urge to smoke ('A') that led me to feel anxious ('C')?
- Answer: 'I must not experience the urge to smoke, and thus I have to get rid of it immediately.'

Brian:
- Question: What was I demanding ('B') about the essay being very difficult ('A') that led me to feel anxious ('C')?
- Answer: 'The essay must be easier.'

Harry:
- Question: What was I demanding ('B') about the discomfort of waiting in the supermarket queue ('A') that led me to feel unhealthily angrily ('C')?
- Answer: 'I must not experience this discomfort.'

---

* These irrational beliefs also explain why you actually went to your SDCZ.

Geraldine:
- Question: What was I demanding ('B') about losing the sense of familiarity if I were to get a more challenging job ('A') that led me to feel anxious ('C')?
- Answer: 'I have to have a sense of familiarity.'

See if you can identify your rigid belief at 'B' by answering the following question in your notebook:

- What was I demanding about my 'A' that led me to feel [provide your unhealthy negative emotion] at 'C'?

Assess your most pertinent extreme belief

As I first discussed in Chapter 2, when you hold a rigid belief you also tend to hold one or more extreme beliefs that lead you to experience a range of disturbed reactions at 'C' if you stay out of your SDCZ when it is healthy for you to do so. There are three such extreme beliefs (awfulizing beliefs, discomfort intolerance beliefs and depreciation beliefs). As I have suggested, after you have identified your rigid belief, I suggest that you select the one extreme belief that best explains your responses at 'C'. This is what Fay, Brian, Harry and Geraldine did, as shown below.

Fay:
- Question: Which extreme belief best fits my experience of feeling anxious about experiencing an urge to smoke?
- Answer: Discomfort intolerance belief: 'I can't tolerate having an urge to smoke.'

Brian:
- Question: Which extreme belief best fits my experience of feeling anxious about the essay being very difficult?
- Answer: Awfulizing belief: 'It would be awful if the essay were very difficult.'

Harry:
- Question: Which extreme belief best fits my experience of feeling unhealthily angry about the discomfort I would experience if I remained in the supermarket queue?

- Answer: Discomfort intolerance belief: 'I can't stand the discomfort of waiting in a queue.'

Geraldine:
- Question: Which extreme belief best fits my experience of being anxious about the sense of unfamiliarity I would experience if I were to get a challenging job?
- Answer: Discomfort intolerance belief: 'I would not be able to put up with the sense of unfamiliarity if I were to get a challenging job.'

Now it is your turn to identify your most pertinent extreme belief. In your notebook, answer the following question:

- Which extreme belief best fits my experience when I felt [provide your unhealthy negative emotion at 'C'] about [provide your 'A'].

In this chapter, I have discussed how you can assess typical episodes when you went to your self-defeating comfort zone (SDCZ) and alternatively when you stayed out of this zone. In the next chapter, I will show you what you need to change to stay out of your SDCZ, but this time while reacting healthily to the adversity at 'A'.

4

How to stay out of your self-defeating comfort zone in the face of adversity without disturbing yourself

In the last chapter, I showed you how to identify the factors at play when you go to your self-defeating comfort zone (SDCZ) in the face of adversity and the factors at play when you stay out of this zone, but are disturbed.

In this chapter, I am going to show you what you need to do to stay out of your SDCZ when it is healthy for you to do so without experiencing disturbed emotions, behaviour and thinking.

In doing this, I suggest that you work with the same specific episode that you selected when carrying out the assessment of the factors associated with your SDCZ. As I did before, I will illustrate my points with reference to the cases of Fay, Brian, Harry and Geraldine.

Step 1: Remind yourself of your goals and keep these to the forefront of your mind

Throughout this part of the process, it is very important that you keep to the forefront of your mind what your goals are with respect to your SDCZ and the reasons why you want to come out and stay out of this zone. Let me remind you of the goals of the four people we are following in this book.

- Fay's goal: 'I want to come out and stay out of my comfort zone by stopping smoking because it will be much better for my health.'
- Brian's goal: 'I want to start tasks that are in my interest to do, rather than put them off.'
- Harry's goal: 'Whenever I have to wait, I want to stay in the situation when it is in my interest to do so.'

- Geraldine's goal: 'Whenever I promise myself that I will look for a new, more challenging job, I want to follow through with it and apply for such positions until I obtain one.'

I do want to stress that these four people kept these goals to the forefront of their minds whenever they encountered situations in which they were vulnerable to going to their SDCZ.

Given the importance that I place on keeping your goals to the forefront of your mind, I suggest that you make use of the goal-setting exercise that you did in the previous chapter and review the answers you gave to the following questions: 'If I came out and stayed out of my SDCZ, how would I change?' 'Why is this important to me?'

Step 2: Specify realistic and healthy ways of responding in the episode in question, having decided to stay out of your SDCZ

It is time to revisit the episode where you went to your SDCZ when it would have been healthy for you to stay out of it. However, as we saw in the previous chapter, had you stayed out of it you would have experienced a set of unhealthy responses underpinned by the irrational beliefs that you held about the adversity at 'A'. These predicted responses also explain why you went to your SDCZ.

In order to stay out of your SDCZ in the episode that you are considering, it is important that you see clearly that you can respond to the adversity at 'A' in healthy, realistic ways rather than in the unhealthy ways already described in your previous assessment (see Chapter 3).

Our four people specified their healthy alternatives to their unhealthy responses as follows:

Fay

When I was offered a cigarette by a co-worker in my tea-break, if I had stayed out of my SDCZ by not taking the cigarette, I would have reacted in the following unhealthy ways to experiencing a strong urge to smoke:

(emotion) = Anxiety.

(behaviour) = Not smoking, getting agitated and then eating chocolate to get rid of the urge to smoke.

(thinking) = 'I'll go mad if I don't get rid of the urge to smoke.'

A more realistic and healthy way of responding to my urge to smoke would be as follows:

(emotion) = Concern.

(behaviour) = Not smoking, feeling uncomfortable, but not doing any-thing to get rid of the urge to smoke. Going back to work at the end of the tea-break.

(thinking) = 'The urge to smoke will reduce in intensity and go away after a while.'

Brian

When I was in my study at 2 p.m. having promised myself that I would start my essay at that time, if I had stayed out of my SDCZ by beginning to work on the essay, I would have reacted in the following unhealthy ways to the thought that the essay would be very difficult:

(emotion) = Anxiety.

(behaviour) = Pacing up and down, engaging in distracting activities, but anxiously.

(thinking) = 'I'll never finish this essay. I'll fail the course.'

A more realistic and healthy way of responding to the thought that the essay would be very difficult would be as follows:

(emotion) = Concern.

(behaviour) = Start working on the essay even though uncomfortable.

(thinking) = 'It may be very difficult and I may need help, but if I persist I will probably finish it. If I work hard and do essays like this one, I will probably pass the course.'

Harry

When I was standing in a long queue at the supermarket check-out, if I had stayed out of my SDCZ and remained in the queue, I would have reacted in the following unhealthy ways to the discomfort of waiting in the queue:

(emotion) = Unhealthy anger.

(behaviour) = Staying in the queue, but increasingly acting in an angry, agitated manner (e.g. swearing and aggressively calling to see the manager).

(thinking) = 'If this queue doesn't move more quickly, I'll explode.'

A more realistic and healthy way of responding to the discomfort of waiting in the queue would be as follows:

(emotion) = Healthy anger.

(behaviour) = Staying in the queue but concentrating on writing emails on my phone or doing Sudoku puzzles.

(thinking) = 'I am going to have a polite word with the manager to open up more check-outs when I get out of this queue.'

Geraldine

When I was looking at jobs online, if I had stayed out of my SDCZ and resolved to apply for jobs I really wanted, I would have reacted in the following unhealthy ways to the loss of familiarity I would experience if I were to get a more challenging job:

(emotion) = Anxiety.

(behaviour) = Playing safe by only applying for a slightly better job that would involve the minimum upheaval, but not applying for jobs I really want which would involve much greater challenge and upheaval.

(thinking) = 'I want a new challenging and fulfilling job, but I will never be able to settle at it.'

A more realistic and healthy way of responding to the unfamiliarity of getting a new, challenging job would be as follows:

(emotion) = Concern.

(behaviour) = Applying for three new jobs that I really want.

(thinking) = 'It will be difficult for me to settle at a new, challenging job, but I will be able to do so eventually.'

Now it's your turn. Take your notebook and list your unhealthy emotional, behavioural and thinking responses to your adversity at 'A', having decided to stay out of your SDCZ. Then list the healthy alternatives to these responses to the same adversity.

Step 3: Identify the rational beliefs that underpin your healthy responses

Throughout this book I have stressed that the beliefs you hold about an adversity have a very important influence on whether you go to your SDCZ or stay out of this zone. In the previous chapters, I have argued that if you hold a set of irrational beliefs (a) you will tend to go to your SDCZ or, should you decide to stay out of this zone, (b) you will feel, act and think in disturbed ways. To a significant degree your comfort zone is designed to protect you from experiencing such disturbance even though it will probably have long-term destructive effects on your physical and mental well-being.

If you are to stay out of your SDCZ and do so without experiencing emotional, behavioural and thinking disturbance, you need a way of doing so. If holding a set of irrational beliefs leads you to go to your SDCZ and to experiencing widespread disturbance if you stay out of it, the RECBT model argues that holding a set of alternative rational beliefs will lead you to stay out of your SDCZ and to do so without disturbance. Indeed, as I will show you, holding an alternative set of rational beliefs will help Fay, Brian, Harry and Geraldine to do just that.

Fay

Question: What would I have to believe (at 'B') to stay out of my SDCZ and not smoke when offered a cigarette by a co-worker in my tea-break, and to have the following consequences (at 'C') about experiencing a strong urge to smoke (at 'A')?

'C' (emotion) = Concern.

(behaviour) = Not smoking, feeling uncomfortable, but not doing anything to get rid of the urge to smoke. Going back to work at the end of the tea-break.

(thinking) = 'The urge to smoke will reduce in intensity and go away after a while.'

Answer:

'B' (flexible belief) = 'I would prefer not to experience the urge to smoke, but I don't have to get rid of it immediately.'

(discomfort tolerance belief) = 'It is hard to tolerate the urge to smoke, but I can tolerate it and it is worth it to me to do so because I want to give up smoking and be healthy.'

Brian

Question: What would I have to believe (at 'B') to stay out of my SDCZ when I was in my study at 2 p.m. having promised myself that I would start my essay at that time and to have the following consequences (at 'C') about the essay being very difficult (at 'A')?

'C' (emotion) = Concern.

(behaviour) = Start working on the essay even though uncomfortable.

(thinking) = 'It may be very difficult and I may need help, but if I persist I will probably finish it'; 'If I work hard and do essays like this one, I will probably pass the course.'

Answer:

'B' (flexible belief) = 'I would like the essay to be easier, but it doesn't have to be so.'

(non-awfulizing belief) = 'It would be bad if the essay were very difficult, but it would not be awful.'

Harry

Question: What would I have to believe (at 'B') to stay out of my SDCZ when I was waiting in the supermarket queue and to have the following healthy consequences (at 'C') about the discomfort of waiting in the queue (at 'A')?

'C' (emotion) = Healthy anger.

(behaviour) = Staying in the queue but concentrating on writing emails on my phone or doing Sudoku puzzles.

(thinking) = 'I am going to have a polite word with the manager to open up more check-outs when I get out of this queue.'

Answer:

'B' (flexible belief) = 'I would prefer not to experience this discomfort, but that does not mean that I must not experience it.'

(discomfort tolerance belief) = 'It is hard for me to stand this discomfort, but it is not unbearable and it is worth bearing because I want the items that I have selected.'

Geraldine

Question: What would I have to believe (at 'B') to stay out of my SDCZ when I was looking online at jobs and to have the following healthy consequences (at 'C') about the unfamiliarity I would experience were I to apply for and get a more challenging job (at 'A')?

'C' (emotion) = Concern.

(behaviour) = Applying for three new jobs online that I really want.

(thinking) = 'It will be difficult for me to settle at a new, challenging job, but I will be able to do so eventually.'

Answer:

'B' (flexible) = 'I would like to experience a sense of familiarity, but I don't have to do so.'

(discomfort tolerance belief) = 'It would be a struggle for me to put up with losing this sense of familiarity, but I can put up with it and it would be worth it for me to do so because I want to further my career.'

Now it's your turn: in your notebook, identify your rational beliefs (at 'B') that would help you to stay out of your SDCZ and to experience healthy responses (at 'C') to the adversity (at 'A'). First list the adversity at 'A', then note the healthy emotional, behavioural and thinking responses you want to experience at 'C'. Now write down the beliefs you would need to hold (give the alternative to your rigid belief and main extreme belief – this will be a flexible belief – and one of the following: a non-awfulizing belief, a discomfort tolerance belief or an acceptance belief).

Step 4: Question your beliefs

With respect to the role of beliefs concerning whether you go to your SDCZ or stay out of it and, if the latter, whether you respond in a disturbed way or a healthy way to the adversity you are facing, I have helped you to see the following.

First, I have shown you that irrational beliefs are largely responsible for you going to your SDCZ in the face of adversity or, if you stay out of it, then they are largely responsible for your disturbed responses at 'C'. Second, I have helped you to see that holding an alternative set of rational beliefs will help you to stay out of your SDCZ and respond healthily to the same adversity.

Hopefully, then, you can see that if you want to learn to come out and stay out of your SDCZ you need to hold a set of rational beliefs rather than a set of irrational beliefs. Assuming that you can see this and that you want to think rationally rather than irrationally about adversity and consequently respond to this adversity healthily without going to your SDCZ, then you need to do two things.

First, you need to see clearly why your rational beliefs are rational and why your irrational beliefs are irrational. I will discuss this point in this section. Second, you will need to act in ways suggested by your rational beliefs rather than by your irrational beliefs, and to do so consistently until you have internalized these rational beliefs. This will be the subject of the following section.

How best to question your beliefs

As I said above, the purpose of questioning your beliefs is for you to see that your irrational beliefs are irrational and that your alternative rational beliefs are rational. While there are a number of ways you can do this, my experience has shown that the most effective and efficient way of doing so through the medium of a self-help book such as this is to take your irrational belief (e.g. your rigid belief) and the rational alternative to this belief (in this case your flexible belief), write these down side by side on a piece of paper or in your notebook, and then ask yourself three questions concerning these two beliefs:

- Which of these beliefs is true and which is false? Then give reasons for your answer.
- Which of these beliefs is logically sensible and which makes no logical sense? Again, give reasons for your answer.
- Which of these beliefs is most helpful to me and which is least helpful to me? Once again, give reasons for your answer.

In Appendices 1–4, I provide suggestions for answers to these questions with respect to your rigid beliefs (and their flexible belief alternatives), your awfulizing beliefs (and their non-awfulizing belief alternatives), your discomfort intolerance beliefs (and their discomfort tolerance belief alternatives) and your depreciation beliefs (and their acceptance belief alternatives).

I suggest that you use these arguments as a guide and then tailor them to the specific irrational and rational beliefs you are questioning. Come up with answers that are compelling and persuasive rather than rote and mechanical.

Once you have answered these three questions concerning your irrational and rational beliefs, make a commitment to weaken your conviction in the former and strengthen your conviction in the latter.

Let me show you how Fay used these arguments to question her beliefs.

Fay

Rigid belief vs flexible belief: Fay first took her rigid belief and her flexible belief and wrote these down on a piece of paper as follows:

Rigid belief = 'I must not experience the urge to smoke.'

Flexible belief = 'I would prefer not to experience the urge to smoke, but that does not mean that I must not experience it or get rid of it immediately.'

Here are the questions she asked herself, with her answers:

- Which of these beliefs is true and which is false? Give reasons for your answer.

My rigid belief is false. The reality is that I have been smoking for many years and therefore even though I want to give up smoking, I will experience an urge to smoke when offered a cigarette. If there were a law of the universe that decreed that I must not experience such an urge then I would not experience it. Therefore, for me to demand that I must not experience such an urge flies in the face of reality.

On the other hand my flexible belief is true. Thus, it is true that I would prefer not to experience the urge to smoke and it is also true that there is no reason why I must not experience it or must get rid of it immediately.

- Which of these beliefs is logically sensible and which makes no logical sense? Again, give reasons for your answer.

My flexible belief is sensible while my rigid belief is not. In neither belief do I want to experience an urge to smoke, but it does not make sense for me to say that I must not experience it because I don't want to do so. However, it does make sense for me to say that just because I have a desire not to have the urge to smoke it does not follow that I must not do so.

- Which of these beliefs is most helpful to you and which is least helpful to you? Once again, give reasons for your answer.

My rigid belief is unhelpful to me because it leads me to go to my SDCZ and smoke when I am offered a cigarette and feel the urge to smoke. Also, if I decide to stay out of my SDCZ and not smoke when I feel the urge to do so, my rigid belief will lead me to feel disturbed, to have very distorted thoughts and to eat to deal with my urge.

By contrast, *my flexible belief is more helpful to me* as it will help me to deal with my urge to smoke without actually smoking and also without eating or feeling disturbed.

Discomfort intolerance belief vs discomfort tolerance belief: Fay then took her discomfort intolerance belief and her discomfort tolerance belief and wrote these down on a piece of paper, as follows:

Discomfort intolerance belief = 'I can't tolerate having an urge to smoke.'

Discomfort tolerance belief = 'It is hard to tolerate the urge to smoke, but I can tolerate it and it is worth it to me to do so, because I want to give up smoking and be healthy.'

She then asked herself the following questions:

- Which of these beliefs is true and which is false? Give reasons for your answer.

My discomfort intolerance belief is false. If it were true that I could not tolerate having the urge to smoke, this would be the case no matter what belief I held about this urge. If I develop the rational belief that I can tolerate the urge to smoke then the urge is not intolerable. Rather, I think it is because of my discomfort intolerance belief.

My discomfort tolerance belief is true because all three elements of this belief are true. Thus, it is true that it is difficult for me to tolerate the urge to smoke. I really enjoy smoking and not doing so is really uncomfortable. However, it is true that, despite this, I can tolerate this urge. There is nothing intrinsically intolerable about this urge. Again, I just think it is when I hold a discomfort intolerance belief about the urge. Finally, it is also true that it is worth it to me to tolerate the urge. Doing so will help me to give up smoking and be healthy.

- Which of these beliefs is logically sensible and which makes no logical sense? Again, give reasons for your answer.

Both of these beliefs acknowledge that it is hard for me to put up with the urge to smoke. This is a non-extreme statement. It does not make sense for me to conclude therefore that I can't tolerate the urge, which is an extreme statement. This is what I do when I hold a discomfort intolerance belief. Jumping from a non-extreme statement to an extreme statement for no good reason is not sensible and therefore *my discomfort intolerance belief is illogical*.

On the other hand, all the elements of my discomfort tolerance belief are non-extreme and I make no such leap to the extreme. Therefore, *my discomfort tolerance belief is logical*.

- Which of these beliefs is most helpful to me and which is least helpful to me? Once again, I need to give reasons for my answer.

The same arguments that I made concerning the helpfulness of my flexible belief and the unhelpfulness of my rigid belief also apply to my discomfort tolerance and intolerance beliefs respectively.

Thus, *my discomfort intolerance belief is unhelpful to me* because it again leads me to go to my SDCZ and smoke when I am offered a cigarette and feel the urge to smoke. Also, if I decide to stay out of my SDCZ and not smoke when I feel the urge to do so, my discomfort intolerance belief will lead me to feel disturbed, to have very distorted thoughts and to eat to deal with my urge.

By contrast, *my discomfort tolerance belief is more helpful to me* as it will help me to deal with my urge to smoke without actually smoking, and also without eating and feeling disturbed.

As a result of questioning her beliefs, Fay could see clearly that her two irrational beliefs were indeed irrational and that the rational alternatives to these beliefs were rational. She was thus easily able to commit herself to strengthening her conviction in her rational beliefs and weakening her conviction in her irrational beliefs. The following section is devoted to the importance of translating this commitment into action.

Step 5: Act on your rational beliefs

If you recall, the therapeutic tradition that this book is based on is known as 'Cognitive Behavioural Therapy' (or CBT). In my view, both the cognitive and behavioural elements are important. Behaviour without cognition (or thinking) is directionless, whereas cognition without behaviour leads to intellectual insight or knowing without conviction. It is this second point I want to address here.

You may think that because you can clearly see (as Fay did) why your rational beliefs are rational and why your irrational beliefs are irrational, you have done all you need to do to come out and stay out of your SDCZ. Nothing could be further from the truth. The insight that you have is known as intellectual insight or what I referred to as knowing without conviction. This type of insight will help you pass an exam on rational and irrational beliefs, but won't, on its own, help you to achieve your goals. When you have intellectual insight on its own you may say things like: 'I understand in my head that I can tolerate the discomfort of not acting on my urge to smoke, but not in my gut.' When you think that intellectual insight is sufficient to lead to change and you find that it isn't, you may say things like, 'I know that I should have been able to tolerate putting up with the urge to smoke, but I couldn't do it.'

This is not to say that intellectual insight isn't important. It is, for without it you would not know what you have to practise. However, it is not sufficient to help you achieve your goals. You need emotional insight (or knowledge with conviction) and you can only gain this by practice. This practice involves you rehearsing your rational beliefs while acting in ways that are in line with these rational beliefs, and doing so consistently over time.

Before you do this, it is important that you understand one point. When you decide not to go to your SDCZ but to stay out of this zone while rehearsing your rational beliefs, the intensity of your discomfort will initially increase. However, if you tolerate this increase in discomfort level, refrain from going to your SDCZ and rehearse your rational beliefs, then after a while the intensity level of your discomfort will peak and then reduce. If you don't grasp this you will go to your SDCZ as soon as your level of discomfort increases, which will only serve to maintain your problem and decrease the chances of you achieving your goals with respect to staying out of your SDCZ while responding healthily to adversity.

Let's see how Fay, Brian, Harry and Geraldine implemented these principles.

Fay

Every time Fay was offered a cigarette, she kept in mind that she wanted to give up smoking and reminded herself of the health benefits of doing so. When she felt the urge to smoke, she reminded herself that she would prefer not to experience this urge, but she did not have to get rid of it quickly. She could tolerate it, and in doing so she could get the experience of not smoking when offered, when she felt the urge to do so and when she saw others smoking. These were her three triggers to smoking.

Within the context of her change programme, Fay made a note of every time she smoked a cigarette and analysed the reasons she did so, using the 'ABC' framework. Then she identified the irrational beliefs that underpinned her smoking behaviour and developed rational beliefs to counteract them. For example, Fay noticed that she was particularly vulnerable to smoking when she had had a hard day at work. She realized that the following irrational belief led her to smoke (i.e. go to her SDCZ): 'Because I have had a hard day at work, I deserve a reward and I must have it as quickly as possible.' Because smoking was an immediate reward for Fay, she smoked. In order to deal with these situations, Fay first developed the following rational alternative to this rigid belief: 'Because I have had a hard day at work, I deserve a reward, but I don't have to have it as quickly as possible.' Fay then was able to think of rewards she could have that did not jeopardize her health (e.g. having a bath, speaking to a friend on the phone, listening to classical music). In doing this, Fay began to break the connection she had made in her mind between smoking and giving herself a reward. [*I will discuss such obstacles to change in the next chapter.*]

Fay also had to deal with the distorted thoughts that she experienced when she did not smoke, and I will show you how she did this and how you can do this in the next section.

In applying these principles, Fay stayed out of her comfort zone (i.e. she did not smoke) whenever she experienced urges to smoke and she did so without overeating or disturbing herself. Consequently, the intensity of Fay's urges to smoke eventually decreased and she is now a non-smoker.

Brian

Brian kept in mind that the reason he wanted to begin tasks rather than put them off was because it was in his interests to do so. These interests were that he would be on top of things rather than stressed about always being behind. Brian determined that he would agree with himself a starting time for these tasks. Whenever he felt the urge to procrastinate, he reminded himself that whatever he decided to do did not have to be easy for him, even though it would be preferable if such conditions were to exist before he started such tasks. He also reminded himself that if such tasks were difficult it would be bad, but hardly the end of the world. Most of the time Brian stayed out of his SDCZ (i.e. procrastination) and in doing so he learned that his predictions that tasks would be very difficult were almost always wrong. Most of the time they were much easier than he anticipated, occasionally they were as difficult and once in a while they were more difficult. However, even when the tasks proved to be difficult the fact that Brian had begun them meant that he had built up a good head of steam to deal with difficult tasks.

Like Fay, Brian occasionally justified his return to his SDCZ, but he learned from these episodes [*which I will discuss in the next chapter*]. He also learned to deal with the distorted thoughts that stayed in his mind even after he had rehearsed his rational beliefs and acted on them. [*I will discuss this issue in the next section.*]

Harry

Harry had a history of leaving queues when it was in his interests to remain in them to get the items or services that he wanted. Leaving queues and thus sparing himself discomfort was his SDCZ. He was determined to learn to remain in queues and do so as patiently as he could. He reminded himself of this goal every time he came upon a queue he had to join in order to get what he wanted.

After he reminded himself of his goal, Harry rehearsed his rational beliefs as he joined the queue. He showed himself that he could tolerate the discomfort of being in the queue, even though he would never like it, and there was no reason why he had to be spared such discomfort. Also, Harry realized that his discomfort level would initially and temporarily increase if he did not leave the queue. He also learned that if he stayed in the situation and practised thinking rationally, this level would eventually tail off. Once he had rehearsed his rational beliefs and had decided to stay in the queue, Harry then occupied his time productively (e.g. by responding to emails on his phone or by doing a Sudoku puzzle).

Harry was particularly vulnerable to leaving a queue if he had stayed in one earlier in the day. He recognized that he held the following irrational belief: 'If I have to stay in a queue, then I must not do so more than once a day.' He challenged this belief and accepted the grim reality that just because he had queued up once it did not follow that he must be spared queuing up again that day. Indeed, he came to recognize that the more queues he joined, the more practice he would get at thinking rationally about the discomfort he felt while remaining in queues. And the more he practised, the better he got at tolerating the discomfort he experienced while waiting in queues. As Harry got better at tolerating this discomfort, the intensity of his discomfort reduced.

Geraldine

Geraldine kept in mind that she was in a rut with respect to her current job. She could do her job very easily and she experienced little or no challenge. She further kept in mind what her goal was, namely: 'Whenever I promise myself that I will look for a new, more challenging job, I want to follow through with it and apply for such positions until I obtain one.' As a result she set herself the target of looking for challenging jobs online and applying for those that she would really like, while rehearsing her rational beliefs about putting up with the unfamiliarity of changing jobs. In doing so, Geraldine began to get interviews for jobs she really wanted. When she felt the urge not to attend these interviews, she recognized that she was thinking irrationally about her anticipated feelings of unfamiliarity and questioned her irrational beliefs forcefully. She resolved to go to every interview that she was offered, and after three months she accepted the offer of a job that she had always dreamed of. On the night before she started this job, she had a sleepless night full of worry based on the same irrational beliefs about unfamiliarity-based discomfort. However, she was prepared for this and rehearsed her alternative rational beliefs until she fell asleep. After a week at her new job, she had settled into it and regretted the time she had wasted remaining in a familiar but unfulfilling job. However, her dominant feeling was far more positive – joy that she had found a job that challenged her and fulfilled her.

Step 6: Dealing with residual distorted thoughts

Once you have begun to rehearse your rational beliefs while acting in ways that are consistent with them, you should bear in mind that your feelings will change, but not immediately. I have already noted that when you do not act to get rid of discomfort the intensity level of this discomfort will initially increase, but will decrease later once you have gained the experience of staying with it and tolerating it.

Something very similar happens with your thinking. In Chapter 2, I showed you that when you hold a set of irrational beliefs these beliefs not only affect how you feel (i.e. your emotions will tend to be negative and unhealthy) and how you act (i.e. your behaviour will largely be unconstructive and goal-defeating), but will also affect how you think, which is the subject of this section.

I showed you in that chapter that when you hold irrational beliefs, then your thinking, particularly when you stay out of your SDCZ, is likely to be highly distorted and skewed to the negative.

Now, when you rehearse your rational beliefs when facing an adversity and you have decided to stay out of your SDCZ, your distorted thinking will linger for a while. It is important that you understand this point. Your distorted thinking is not like a light bulb that you can turn off instantly. It is more akin to the after-image that stays on your retina for a while after you have stared at a very bright light.

Once you have understood this phenomenon it is important that you accept the existence of such thinking, respond to it briefly and then let it be in your mind without (a) attempting to get rid of it or (b) engaging with it. If you do this, then such thinking will fade from your mind, particularly if you are acting in a way that is consistent with your rational beliefs.

If you try to get rid of such thinking you will only succeed at keeping these thoughts in your mind. We know from psychological experiments that attempts to suppress or eliminate unwanted thoughts only serve to keep such thoughts in your mind. Think, for example, of a polar bear and then try to suppress all thoughts of this animal. You will see that the opposite effect will occur and that you will have more thoughts about the polar bear.

As I pointed out above, even though you are rehearsing your rational beliefs you will still have highly distorted thoughts that stem from your ingrained irrational beliefs. I suggest that you respond to these thoughts, but then accept them without engaging with them further. Further engagement will only serve to keep such distorted thoughts in your mind and thus is to be avoided as much as possible.

Let's see how our four people dealt with the residual distorted thoughts that stemmed from their irrational beliefs when they were actively involved in rehearsing their rational beliefs and acting in ways that were consistent with these beliefs.

Fay

When Fay decided not to act on her urge to smoke but to rehearse her rational beliefs with reference to that urge, initially she still experienced the following distorted thought that stemmed from her urge-related irrational beliefs: 'I'll go mad if I don't get rid of the urge to smoke.' Initially, Fay questioned that thought and concluded that it was highly unlikely that she would go mad if she refrained from smoking. Having responded to that thought, Fay then accepted that this thought would stay in her mind as she refrained from smoking, and although the thought was compelling, she did not engage with it once she had responded to it, as detailed above. As she did this, Fay thought more realistically about her urge to smoke, thus: 'The urge to smoke will reduce in intensity and go away after a while.'

Brian

When Brian decided to start work on his essay despite the fact that it might prove very difficult and rehearsed his rational belief about its difficulty, he still tended to think in a distorted way that stemmed from his irrational belief, thus: 'I'll never finish this essay. I'll fail the course.'

Initially, Brian questioned this thought and showed himself that even if the essay was very difficult, it did not follow that he would never finish it, nor that he would fail the course. However, Brian also recognized that even though his distorted thoughts stemmed from his irrational beliefs, they would still stay in his mind despite the fact that he was rehearsing his rational beliefs and that he had responded to such thoughts. He got on with his essay while accepting the presence of these thoughts, and tried neither to suppress them nor to respond to them further. In time his distorted thoughts faded from his mind and he was able to access the following realistic and balanced thoughts: 'The essay may be very difficult and I may need help, but if I persist I will probably finish it. If I work hard and do essays like this one, I will probably pass the course.'

Harry

When Harry decided to remain in queues despite the fact that it was an uncomfortable experience for him and rehearsed his rational belief about such discomfort, he still tended to think in a distorted way that stemmed from his irrational beliefs, thus: 'If this queue doesn't move more quickly I'll explode.' Initially, Harry questioned this thought and showed himself that it was highly unlikely that he would explode if he stayed in the queue, no matter how uncomfortable he was. However, Harry also recognized that even though this distorted thought stemmed from his irrational beliefs, he would still think it even though he was rehearsing his rational beliefs, and that he had responded to the thought. He remained in the queue and either did a Sudoku puzzle or wrote emails on his phone while accepting the presence of this thought, and tried neither to suppress it nor respond to it further. As he did so, this distorted thought faded from his mind and he was able to access the following realistic and balanced thought instead: 'I am not going to explode. Rather, I am going to have a polite word with the manager to open up more check-outs when I get out of this queue.'

Geraldine

When Geraldine decided to apply for jobs that she really wanted despite the fact that this would lead to a sense of unfamiliarity and rehearsed her rational belief about such unfamiliarity, she still tended to think in a distorted way that stemmed from her irrational belief, thus: 'I want a new challenging and fulfilling job, but I will never be able to settle at it.' Initially, Geraldine questioned this thought and showed herself that it would be highly unlikely that she would never settle at a new challenging job. However, she also recognized that even though this distorted thought stemmed from her irrational belief, it would still be in her mind despite the fact that she was rehearsing her rational beliefs, and that she had responded to the thought. She kept applying for jobs that she really wanted while accepting the presence of this thought and tried neither to suppress it nor to respond to it further. As she did so, this distorted thought faded from her mind and she was able to access the following realistic and balanced thought instead: 'It will be difficult for me to settle at a new, challenging job, but I will be able to do so eventually.'

When you decide to stay out of your SDCZ, remember the following points about dealing with highly distorted thoughts that are skewed to the negative that accompany your decision.

1 Understand that these thoughts stem from irrational beliefs.
2 Appreciate that they will remain in your mind for a while even when you are rehearsing your rational beliefs.
3 Respond to such thoughts, but do so only once per episode. To do so any more often risks you re-engaging with such thoughts.
4 Accept the presence of these thoughts.
5 Realize that you may experience the urge to suppress such thoughts. Do not act on such urges.
6 Also, realize that you may experience the urge to re-engage with such thoughts. Again, do not do so.
7 Continue to act in ways that are consistent with your rational beliefs as you mentally rehearse such beliefs.
8 Understand and discover that these distorted thoughts will fade from your mind if you implement the aforementioned steps. You will then be able to access and focus on alternative thoughts that are realistic and balanced.

So far in this book I have dealt with the major steps that you need to take to understand the factors that lead you to go to your SDCZ, and what you need to do to come out and stay out of this zone while responding healthily to adversity. In the next chapter, I will discuss the major obstacles that you may well encounter as you strive to stay out of your SDCZ and what you need to do to deal with these obstacles.

5

Identifying and dealing with obstacles to continued progress

Introduction

This book is based on the central idea that when you stay in or go to your comfort zone when it is not healthy for you to do so, then the main reason that you do so is because, at that point, you hold a set of irrational beliefs about the adversity that you face or think you face. You basically believe that you have to maintain comfort or gain immediate escape from discomfort and you act on this idea.

As I have shown you, it follows from this that if you want to stay out of your SDCZ in the face of this adversity (or come out of it if you have gone there) and you want to react healthily, it is important that you hold a set of rational beliefs. Here you basically believe that while you might want to remain comfortable or gain immediate escape from discomfort, you don't need to do this and it is healthier in the longer term if you face the discomfort and get on with achieving your goals. In order to be truly convinced of this latter idea, you need to act in ways that are consistent with it and do so with regularity.

However, like the path of true love, the path towards coming out and staying out of your self-defeating comfort zone is rarely smooth, and in this chapter I will identify some of the major obstacles that you may well encounter along this path and show you how you can deal with them.

Develop the 'I'm worth it' philosophy

One of the key elements of coming out and staying out of your SDCZ is to recognize the self-defeating nature of this zone and the positive long-term effects to be gained from staying out of it. Keeping these effects in mind serves as a motivational counterpoint to the seductive call of your comfort zone. In short, you need to keep in the forefront of your mind the idea that it is worth it to you to come out of and stay out of your SDCZ.

However, even if you do this, you may not consider that you are worth doing it for! If you think that this applies to you, it is important that you ask yourself why you think you are not worth the effort that you will need to make in order to come out and stay out of your SDCZ. Whatever reason you give yourself (e.g. 'I am not worth it because I am fat . . . because I have not treated my parents well over the years . . . because I had an abortion', etc.), what is happening here is that you are focusing on something negative about you or your experience and depreciating your entire self as a result. Instead, you need to accept yourself as an unrateable, complex, fallible human being who has strengths and weaknesses, faults and good points, and accept that the negative aspect of yourself you are focusing on (which you may well need to address) is not sufficient reason for you to consider that you are not worth making the effort for with respect to coming out of and staying out of your SDCZ.

There used to be an advertisement for L'Oréal, the cosmetics company, where in answer to the implied question, 'Why should I take care of myself and use these products?' came the answer, 'Because I'm worth it.' In RECBT, we say that you are worth it because you are a unique, complex, fallible human being who is constantly in flux.

If you struggle with this concept to the extent that you will not embark on work to come out of and stay out of your SDCZ, then I suggest that you first read my book entitled *How to Accept Yourself* (Sheldon Press, 1999) and apply the insights you will find there. Then, when you consider that you are worth making the effort for, come back to this book and apply the insights that you find here.

More speed, less haste

When you embark on any self-change programme such as this one, it is important that you go at a speed that will help you achieve your goals. Some people, particularly those whose SDCZ protects them from the effects of impatience, may be impatient for change and will try to rush through the steps described in this book. They believe, for example, that they must overcome their problem with their SDCZ as quickly as possible and they can't bear the discomfort of not doing so. If you hold this belief, as mentioned above, you will rush through the steps outlined so far in this book. The consequence of doing this is that you will not fully grasp the meaning of your rational beliefs or give yourself the chance to act consistently in ways that will serve to strengthen your conviction in these beliefs. As a result, you will tend to have only intellectual understanding concerning why your irrational beliefs are irrational and your rational beliefs are rational.

To overcome this obstacle, you need to show yourself that while it would be good if you overcame your problem with your SDCZ as quickly as possible, it is not necessary for you to do so, and that you can tolerate the discomfort of going more slowly than you would ideally prefer. In doing this, you will take care to digest properly the information contained in all the steps that I have covered and to undertake a carefully designed programme to act in ways that are consistent with your rational beliefs. In this way, you will maximize the chances of getting the most out of this book. As the saying goes: 'More haste, less speed!' Or as I say in this context: 'More speed, less haste!'

Learn to walk before you run

Some people really get enthused with the idea of coming out and staying out of their self-defeating comfort zones, so much so that they bite off more than they can chew and try to stay out of all their SDCZs at once. This rarely works since they need to learn important skills, as outlined in this book, and such skill learning takes time and is best done in one area and then generalized to other areas later. If you try to deal with all the problems with respect to your comfort zone at once, you will probably feel overwhelmed and get discouraged when you don't make the kind of progress you hoped for.

So my advice is: learn to walk before you run. Select one SDCZ that you want to stay out of and apply the skills that you have learned from this book to that one area. Then, when you have made significant progress in that area, generalize your learning to another area. The more skilled you become at staying out of your SDCZs, the more you will be able to pick up speed and make appropriate changes across the board.

Dispel the 'right conditions' myth

One of the major obstacles to dealing productively with your self-defeating comfort zone concerns the idea that you need certain conditions to exist before you tackle these problems. Here are some examples of what I mean:

- 'I must be in the right frame of mind to deal with my problem with impatience.'
- 'I must feel motivated to give up smoking.'
- 'I need to feel anxious to work on the essay that I have been putting off.'

In all of these cases, people are insisting that certain conditions exist before they strive to come out of and stay out of their SDCZ. As a result, they postpone addressing their comfort zone problems until the demanded conditions exist.

The way to deal with this obstacle is to acknowledge that while it would be better if the preferred conditions were in place before you address your comfort zone problem, it is not necessary for them to exist and you can address your problem in their absence. Thus:

- 'I would prefer to be in the right frame of mind to deal with my problem with impatience, but this is not necessary. I can deal with my impatience without being in the right frame of mind.'
- 'It would be better if I felt motivated to give up smoking before I did so, but this is not a necessary condition for smoking cessation. I can give up without the feeling of motivation as long as I am clear why I want to give up.'
- 'I don't need to feel anxious to work on the essay that I have been putting off. I can do so without the feeling of anxiety and it would be better for me if I did.'

Learn from lapses

When you commit yourself to working to come out and stay out of your SDCZ, then it is important for you to realize that, as I have said, like the path of true love the path towards dealing with your comfort zone problem is rarely smooth. In this context, it means grasping the idea that you will experience lapses. A lapse might be defined in this context as 'a non-significant and temporary return to your SDCZ' once you have made progress at staying out of it. By contrast, a relapse is a more enduring and significant return to a problem state.

When you experience a lapse, this may be an obstacle to progress if you hold an irrational belief about the lapse. Here, you demand that you must not experience a lapse and hold one or more of the following extreme beliefs that are derived from this rigid belief:

- 'It's terrible if I experience a lapse.'
- 'Experiencing a lapse is intolerable.'
- 'If I experience a lapse I'm a failure.'

If you hold a set of irrational beliefs about a lapse you will disturb yourself about it and this disturbance will make it quite difficult for you to stand back, reflect on your experience and learn from the lapse. You need to address your irrational beliefs and develop alternative flexible beliefs about lapsing, thus: 'I would much prefer it if I did not lapse, but I am not immune from doing so, and nor do I have to be so immune.' Once you have developed this flexible belief, you will then be able to develop one or more of the following non-extreme beliefs that are derived from the flexible belief:

- 'It's bad if I experience a lapse, but it's not terrible.'
- 'Experiencing a lapse is hard to endure, but it's not intolerable.'
- 'If I experience a lapse I'm not a failure. I'm a fallible human being who has failed on this occasion to stay out of my SDCZ.'

Once you develop a rational set of beliefs, you can learn from your lapse by assessing it using the 'ABC' model that I outlined in Chapter 2. Use the following scheme:

1 Describe the situation you were in when you lapsed.
2 Describe your lapse by outlining the behaviour that took you into your SDCZ.
3 What unhealthy negative emotion would you have experienced if you had stayed out of your SDCZ?
4 If you experienced this disturbed negative emotion, what were you most disturbed about in the situation you were in?
5 Identify your rigid belief and the one extreme belief that best represented your experience.
6 Identify your alternative flexible belief and your alternative non-extreme belief.
7 Question your rigid belief and your flexible belief and your extreme or non-extreme belief.
8 Resolve to act on your rational beliefs.

Identify and deal with your vulnerability factors

In the context of helping yourself to come out and stay out of your SDCZ, a vulnerability factor is literally a factor to which you are vulnerable in the sense that you respond to it by returning to your SDCZ.

Such vulnerability factors can be external (e.g. when others tempt you to engage in behaviour that represents a return to your SDCZ) and/or internal (e.g. when you experience urges to engage in behaviour that represents a return to your SDCZ).

As far as you can, it is important to deal with your vulnerability factors according to a principle that I have termed 'challenging, but not overwhelming'. This means planning to face a vulnerability factor duly prepared when doing so is a challenge for you, but not overwhelming for you. In this way, you don't go too slowly and deprive yourself of the opportunity of tolerating any discomfort, but you also don't go too quickly and find yourself in a situation that you just can't handle.

Having said this, you cannot completely control your environment and you may find yourself in a situation to which you are vulnerable with respect to going to your SDCZ that you don't have the present capacity to deal with. If this happens, learn from the situation in the same way as you would learn from a lapse (as detailed above).

When planning to deal with your vulnerability factors, I suggest that you take the following steps, which I will illustrate with the case of Fay.

1 *Specify your vulnerability factor.* Fay: Being offered a cigarette when drinking a cup of coffee.
2 *Specify the set of rational beliefs that would help you to deal with this factor.* Fay: 'I would like the other person to accept that I don't want a cigarette and not to think less of me when I refuse, but he or she doesn't have to do what I want. If someone does think less of me I can tolerate it.'
3 *Develop a shorthand version of these beliefs to use in 'vulnerable' situations.* A full expression of rational beliefs can be fairly lengthy (as demonstrated in the example above), and thus you may wish to develop a shorthand version to rehearse as you approach your vulnerable situations and to use while in these situations. Fay: 'I can tolerate the other person thinking less of me.'
4 *Develop a hierarchy of situations that embody your vulnerable factor.* It helps to specify a variety of situations that embody your factor and then arrange them in order from the least challenging to the most challenging. This gives you a direction in which to deal with your vulnerable factor in a sensible, stepwise manner.
    Fay developed the following hierarchy, which went from most challenging to least challenging:
    (a) Going round for coffee to my friend Lisa's house where she will be with my other friends, Sarah and Fiona. They all smoke and will put me under quite a bit of pressure to smoke.
    (b) Going out for coffee with Judy. She will want me to join her for a cigarette to ease her own guilt.
    (c) Going out for coffee with an acquaintance who offers me a cigarette.
    (d) Going out for coffee with someone I don't know who offers me a cigarette.
5 *Face your hierarchy items in reality.* The next step is for you to face your hierarchy items in reality while rehearsing the shorthand version of your rational beliefs. You might want to do this using imagery before you do so in reality. However, it is the actual

real-life practice which will enable you to overcome your vulnerability to your vulnerability factors!

After you have faced one of your vulnerability factors, review what
happened and what you learned from what happened, trouble-
shooting any problems along the way.

Fay

Fay was able to face all but the most difficult item on her hierarchy
without using imagery, and she did very well in not accepting a cigarette even when Judy put her under a lot of pressure to ease her guilt by
joining her in smoking. However, even though she rehearsed in imagery
dealing with going round to Lisa's house, when it came to it she relented
and smoked a cigarette when put under pressure by Lisa and her other
friends.

On reflecting on this experience, Fay considered that what she found difficult to deal with was being accused of being 'boring' by Lisa when she
refused the offer of a cigarette. It was then that she took the cigarette, to
prove to Lisa and her other friends that she was not boring.

Fay then developed a more persuasive rational belief to deal with the
accusation of being boring. She arranged another coffee meeting at
Lisa's and was able to refuse the offer of a cigarette while rehearsing her
new rational belief (i.e. 'I am not boring just because Lisa thinks I am').

Identify and respond to your rationalizations

One of the biggest obstacles to coming out and staying out of your
SDCZ concerns your use of rationalizations. A rationalization, in
this context, is a plausible but untrue reason that you give yourself
to justify your behaviour that led you to go to your SDCZ. However,
it is important to recognize that a rationalization does not actually
explain your behaviour. It justifies it.

Here are some examples of rationalizations.

- 'I smoked because I had a really bad day at work' (Fay).
- 'I didn't begin my essay because I felt tired' (Brian).
- 'I left the supermarket queue because I was late for an appoint-
  ment' (Harry).

- 'I didn't apply for challenging jobs online because I was not in the mood' (Geraldine).

In order to deal with rationalizations you need to take the following steps, which I illustrate with the case of Brian:

1 *Be honest with yourself.* Unless you are honest with yourself you will not deal effectively with your rationalizations. A rationalization is basically a lie, and the first step in dealing with a lie is to admit that it is a lie.

2 *Identify the reason for your rationalization.* Once you have accepted that the explanation you have given yourself to account for SDCZ-seeking behaviour is really a rationalization, you need to ascertain the reason why you used it.

   Brian was honest with himself and realized that the reason he used tiredness as an excuse for not beginning his essay was that he did not want to admit at that moment that he had a problem.

3 *Identify the irrational belief behind the reason for the rationalization, question it and develop a rational alternative to this belief.* Quite often you hold an implicit irrational belief that underpins the reason you used the rationalization. You may find it useful to ask yourself: 'What was I demanding with respect to the reason for my rationalization?' Or you could identify the main extreme belief that is derived from your rigid belief. When you have done this, question this rigid belief and/or extreme belief and develop a flexible and/or non-extreme alternative belief.

   In Brian's case, he was demanding that he had to be comfortable at that moment and that he could not bear being uncomfortable. Admitting that he had a problem beginning his essay would have meant feeling uncomfortable. Rather than admit this, Brian said that the reason he did not start the essay was because he was 'tired'.

   Brian showed himself that while it would be better if he was not uncomfortable while recognizing that he had a problem beginning his essay, he did not have to be spared such discomfort. He could tolerate it and it was worth it for him to do so.

4 *Resolve to act on your rational beliefs.* Once you have developed your rational beliefs concerning the real reason you stayed in

or went to your SDCZ, then you need to act on it consistently. In this context, this means that as soon as you recognize your rationalization, you rehearse and act on your rational belief about the relevant adversity.

Every time Brian found himself resisting beginning a task because he was 'tired' he reminded himself that this was a rationalization rather than a good reason for not starting it. Instead, he showed himself that he could tolerate the discomfort both of starting the task and of the task possibly being very difficult, and he backed this up with action by immediately beginning the task. As Brian did this over time, he found himself using rationalizations far less frequently than before.

Deal with the *mañana* attitude

When you say that you will do something tomorrow rather than today (assuming that it is in your best interest to do it today), then you are using what is perhaps the most frequent excuse for not working to come out of and stay out of your SDCZ. When you tell yourself that you will do it tomorrow, you often use a rationalization to support your decision. Here are some common examples:

- 'I am not in the mood right now, so I'll do it tomorrow (when I will be in the mood).'
- 'I am not motivated right now, so I'll do it tomorrow (when I will be motivated).'
- 'I don't have the energy right now, so I'll do it tomorrow (when I will have the energy).'

As you will see from these examples, the person is demanding that certain conditions exist for him (in this case) to take action to come out of his SDCZ and has the magical idea that the stated condition will exist when he does the task tomorrow. Of course, when tomorrow comes the chances are that the required conditions will again be absent, so the *mañana* attitude will again be applied. Indeed, it may be that, for people who have the *mañana* attitude, the very act of doing something that they ideally don't want to do, but is in their best interests to do, means that their required conditions will be absent. Thus, if you don't want to do something, you are unlikely to be in the right frame of mind to do it, for example.

The antidote to the *mañana* attitude is the Nike principle: do it now! This means that assuming you have ascertained that it is in your interest to do a task at a particular time, then you do it at that time without any internal debate or without arranging an external disruption. If you find yourself beginning to operate according to the *mañana* attitude and starting to justify postponement, then do the following:

- Acknowledge what you are doing.
- Recognize that it would be desirable to have your conditions in place before you begin the task, but that it is not necessary to have them in place.
- Choose to begin the task without the desired conditions.

Recruit help from others

Helping yourself to come out and stay out of your SDCZ can be a lonely enterprise. You may, of course, prefer to help yourself without assistance, in which case recruiting help from others is not something you would wish to consider. However, you may value the help and support of others as you work towards coming out and staying out of your SDCZ. If this is the case, you may struggle if you don't have others to help or support you when the going gets tough for you. In this case, seriously consider recruiting others to assist you.

Other people can help you in the following ways:

1 They can encourage you (e.g. by showing an interest in your progress and providing support when the going gets tough).
2 If they know what your goals are, they can help you to achieve them (e.g. if they know that you want to quit smoking they can refrain from offering you cigarettes).
3 They can intervene when others wittingly or unwittingly invite you to act in a way that leads you back to your SDCZ.

You do need to give careful thought to the people you are going to recruit to help you. They need to care about your welfare and be prepared to do what you ask them to do to help you to achieve your goals. Once you have decided on whom to ask, make sure that you clearly tell them what your goals are and what you want them to do to help you to achieve these goals. If you are unsure about asking others to help you, remember this adage: 'You alone can do it, but you don't have to do it alone.'

Deal with relapse

As I explained earlier, a relapse involves you going back to square one after you have made some progress at working to come out and stay out of your self-defeating comfort zone. This means one of two things. First, it may mean that you have not implemented any steps to deal with the lapses you experience and the vulnerability factors that often underpin such lapses. Second, it may mean that the steps that you have employed have proven to be unsuccessful.

If you have relapsed then I suggest that you do the following:

1 Accept yourself as a fallible human being who has either not responded to lapses or has been unsuccessful in the steps that you have taken to deal with them. There is no law that dictates that you must not relapse. If you have, you have.
2 Take the horror out of relapse. You can prove that relapse is inconvenient for you. It means that you need to start from scratch and do the work that you need to do to come out and stay out of your SDCZ. But horrible? Hardly! As Smokey Robinson's mother used to tell her son: 'From the day you are born till you ride in the hearse, there's nothing so bad that it couldn't be worse.' So put your relapse in perspective and take the horror out of it, but not the badness.
3 Once you have undisturbed yourself about your relapse, the third step that you need to take is to understand why it happened.

When you took steps to deal with lapses, but they proved unsuccessful

If you employed steps to deal with the lapses that you experienced, you need to understand why they were not successful. You may find the following tips helpful:

- Check whether you reminded yourself of your goals. If not, do so and proceed.
- If you did, check whether you accurately identified the adversity at 'A' to which you responded by going to your SDCZ. If not, do so and proceed.
- If you did, check whether you identified the irrational beliefs that accounted for you going to your SDCZ. If not, do so and proceed.
- If you did, check whether you developed rational alternatives to your rational beliefs. If not, do so and proceed.
- If you did, check whether you questioned these beliefs persuasively and resolved to act on your rational beliefs. If not, do so and proceed.
- If you did, check whether you acted in ways that were in line with your rational beliefs and not in line with your irrational beliefs. If not, do so and proceed.
- If you did, check whether you acted in line with your rational beliefs consistently. If not, do so and proceed.
- If you did, then it might be useful to have a face-to-face consultation with an RECBT therapist who will be able to help you to pinpoint where you have been going wrong.

I suggest that you use the above tips with each of your vulnerability factors.

When you did not take steps to deal with lapses

If you did not take any steps to deal with your lapses, you need to understand why, since this will almost certainly lead to relapse now and in the future.

You might find the following tip helpful.

- Do you hold the rigid belief that your progress at coming out and staying out of your SDCZ must be smooth and that you must not experience any lapses? If so, you need to challenge this belief since it will almost certainly lead to relapse. Show yourself that while it would be nice if you experienced no lapses, to some degree this would be going against the human condition, since it may be argued that humans are 'lapsing organisms'. This means that no matter how much progress you make towards coming out and staying out of your SDCZ, you will always be prone to lapsing, and if you are not prepared for this you will take no steps to deal with lapses when they occur – a sure-fire route to relapse. So, accept the grim reality that lapses will, in all probability, happen and take steps to minimize the likelihood of these happening, and learn from them when they do occur.

In addition, you may profit from asking yourself the following question:

- What conditions do I think must be present before I deal with my lapses? (I suggest that you consult the section entitled: 'Dispel the "right conditions" myth' presented earlier in this chapter; see p. 63).

Consult a professional if you are stuck

If you have tried everything that I have suggested in this chapter and you find that you still can't make sustained progress towards coming out and staying out of your SDCZ, then I suggest that you consult an RECBT therapist, who will be able to help you pinpoint the reason(s) for you not being able to overcome your obstacles to change and suggest ways in which you can address these obstacles. Remember, there is no shame in seeking such help. It is possible that you may have one or more subtle and difficult-to-spot obstacles to change which, try as you might, you just can't identify. Consulting an RECBT therapist for a set number of sessions will avail you of the services of a skilled professional who has been trained to assess such elusive factors and to assist you in fine-tuning your self-help efforts. Regard such a person as more of a consultant than a therapist, since this is what he or she would be.

In this chapter, I have suggested a number of ways that you can address and transcend common obstacles to change as you are working to come out and stay out of your SDCZ. In the next chapter, I will show you how to apply all the ideas presented so far to problems associated with maintaining comfort.

6

Dealing with problems associated with maintaining comfort

Introduction

In Chapter 1, I distinguished between two different types of self-defeating comfort zones:

- Maintaining comfort: here you are in your comfort zone and you remain in it to avoid engaging in activities that you find uncomfortable, but that would help you achieve your goals if you engaged with them.
- Eliminating discomfort: here you experience discomfort, and although it is in your interest to tolerate this discomfort, you instead seek to eliminate it.

In this chapter, I will focus on the three main problems that people experience when they maintain comfort when it is not healthy for them to do so. In the following chapter, I will deal with the three main problems people experience when they eliminate discomfort when it is not healthy for them to do so.

In both this chapter and the next, I will discuss the main features of these problems and provide general guidance on how to deal with them. In doing so, I will draw on the material I discussed in Chapters 2–5.

In this chapter – which focuses on problems which reflect your attempts to maintain comfort when it is not healthy for you to do so – I will consider the following three problems:

1 procrastination;
2 being in a rut;
3 lack of persistence.

Dealing with procrastination

When you procrastinate you put off till later something that is in your best interests to do today. Procrastination is a good example of what psychologists call an approach–avoidance conflict. Before you decide to do the task, you are in a comfortable state. Then, when you approach the task, you experience discomfort which you eliminate by avoiding starting the task. While this gets rid of the more acute discomfort that you would feel (or that you predict you would feel) if you began the task, you experience a less intense feeling of discomfort because you know it would have been better if you had started the task and you also know that you need to do it at some point. In order to deal with this form of discomfort, you justify your actions by the use of one or more rationalizations that I discussed in Chapter 5 (see pp. 67–9).

You also may engage in what I call pseudo-work to deal with your feelings of discomfort. This is work that can be seen as related to the task, but that is actually not a part of it. Examples of pseudo-work include:

- tidying your workspace;
- preparing your work materials;
- doing more research (which you don't need to do before you begin the task);
- dealing with other tasks that you think need to be done before you begin work on the task at hand.

While rationalizations are basically thoughts and pseudo-work is basically behaviour, they both serve to convince you that you are not, in fact, procrastinating. In the case of rationalizations and some forms of pseudo-work, you show yourself that you have a legitimate reason for not beginning the task, and in other forms of pseudo-work you show yourself that you are working on the task when in fact you are not.

Steps to deal with procrastination

While a full consideration of how to deal with procrastination warrants a book on its own (e.g. see my book for Sheldon Press entitled

Overcoming Procrastination, published in 2000), let me outline a number of steps to deal with this ubiquitous problem.

Acknowledge that you have a problem with procrastination

Unless you admit to yourself that you have a problem with procrastination, it is unlikely that you will deal with it. If you have a problem with procrastination and are loath to admit it, it may well be that you are ashamed of having this problem. If so, this is how to deal with your shame. Recognize that even if you see your procrastination problem as a weakness, you are not a weak person. Rather, you are a fallible human being with a problem, and a problem that you can address.

Specify your goals

Once you have acknowledged that you have a problem, it is important that you are clear with yourself concerning what your goals are with respect to the tasks you have been procrastinating on. In deciding on your goals, be realistic in your judgements about how long the tasks you need to do will take you and be specific on your starting time.

Identify the feeling that you would experience if you were on the brink of starting the task

When you procrastinate, you are avoiding something. It may thus be difficult for you to identify the feeling that you would experience if you were to start the task. As a result, you need to imagine yourself about to start the task and guess how you would feel if you did. Are you feeling anxious, depressed, unhealthily angry, for example? Take an educated guess and make a note of this emotion on a sheet of paper or in your notebook.

Identify what you are avoiding

As I pointed out at the beginning of this chapter, procrastination is an example of an approach–avoidance conflict. When you put off doing a task, you are avoiding something. Take your hypothesized feeling (e.g. anxiety) and ask yourself the following question: 'If I was just about to start the task and I felt anxious, what would I be most anxious about?' Your answer indicates what you are avoiding.

There are two other ways of discovering what you are avoiding. The first is simply to ask yourself: 'What am I avoiding with respect to the task?' The second is to use the 'magic question' technique. Here, ask yourself the question: 'What condition would I need to be present in order for me to begin the task?' Very frequently, the opposite of this condition is what you are avoiding. For example, Brian asked himself this question: 'What condition would I need to be present for me to begin my essay?' His answer was: 'That the essay would not be very difficult.' Thus, Brian was avoiding the idea that the essay would be very difficult.

Here are some common conditions that people avoid when they procrastinate:

- feeling discomfort (this condition is almost always present in the minds of those who procrastinate and can exist on its own or with one of the following conditions);
- uncertainty that I will be able to do the task;
- failing the task;
- the task being very difficult (as was the case with Brian);
- the idea that doing the task means that I am being controlled by others;
- not being ready to do the task;
- not feeling motivated to do the task;
- boredom.

Identify your irrational beliefs and their rational alternatives

It is a hallmark of Rational-Emotive Cognitive Behavioural Therapy or RECBT (the approach on which this book is based) that the negative conditions you avoid when you procrastinate do not, on their own, explain why you procrastinate. Rather, your procrastination is based largely on the beliefs that you hold about these conditions. This is actually quite an optimistic standpoint. For, if your procrastination was really determined by you lacking the feeling of motivation to do the task, you would have to find a way to get that feeling or wait for it to come before you started the task. However, if your beliefs about not feeling motivated largely determine your procrastination, then by changing your beliefs you can start the task even though you lack this feeling.

As I have shown you in Chapters 2 and 3, the reason you stay in or go to your SDCZ is because you hold a set of irrational beliefs about the negative conditions that you face or that you think you will face if you begin a task. If you remember, there are two types of irrational beliefs: rigid beliefs and three extreme beliefs that are derived from these rigid beliefs, that is, awfulizing beliefs, discomfort intolerance beliefs and depreciation beliefs. My suggestion is that, as a matter of course, you identify the rigid belief that you hold about the negative condition that you would like to avoid and the one extreme belief that best matches your experience. Here are some tips to help you select your main extreme belief:

- If the presence of the negative condition poses a threat to your self-esteem then your main extreme belief is likely to be a self-depreciation belief.
- If you are unhealthily angry towards someone you deem responsible for the negative condition, then your main belief is likely to be an other-depreciation belief.
- Otherwise, your main extreme belief will be an awfulizing belief, a discomfort intolerance belief or a life-depreciation belief.

When you have selected your rigid belief and the main extreme belief that, taken together, explain your procrastination, then you need to identify their rational alternatives. Thus:

- Identify your flexible belief alternative to your rigid belief.
- Identify your non-awfulizing belief alternative to your awfulizing belief.
- Identify your discomfort tolerance belief alternative to your discomfort intolerance belief.
- Identify your acceptance belief alternative to your depreciation belief.

Question your beliefs and commit yourself to those that help you to achieve your goals

Once you have your rigid belief and its flexible belief alternative and your main extreme belief and its non-extreme belief alternative, you are ready to question them. As I suggested in Chapter 3, when you question your beliefs you take your rigid and flexible beliefs together and ask yourself which is true and which is false, which is logical and which is illogical, and which is helpful and which is unhelpful, giving reasons for each of your answers.

In Appendices 1–4, I provide suggestions for answers to these questions with respect to your rigid beliefs (and their flexible belief alternatives), your awfulizing beliefs (and their non-awfulizing belief alternatives), your discomfort intolerance beliefs (and their discomfort intolerance belief alternatives) and your depreciation beliefs (and their acceptance belief alternatives).

The purpose of this questioning process is to help you to see clearly why your irrational beliefs are irrational and why your rational beliefs are rational. This insight is known as intellectual insight and it should help you to commit yourself to the set of beliefs that will help you to achieve your goals, namely your rational beliefs.

Take action while rehearsing your rational beliefs

As I mentioned above, the purpose of questioning your beliefs is to understand why your irrational beliefs are irrational and why your rational beliefs are rational, and to commit yourself to strengthening your conviction in the former and weakening your conviction in the latter. The way you do this is by taking action in ways that are in line with your rational beliefs and not in line with your irrational beliefs, and to take such action consistently. It is also helpful to rehearse your rational beliefs (especially shorthand versions of them) before you take action, while you are taking action and, if relevant, after you have taken action.

For example, you can remind yourself that you don't have to feel motivated to begin a task, and then begin it even though you are not feeling motivated. Or you can start a task even though you don't know whether you can do it, since you don't have to have such assurance. The important point to remember when you are addressing problems with procrastination is that you can take action even when desirable conditions are absent, but that when you make such conditions necessary you will procrastinate.

Understand and accept initial increases in disturbed functioning

When you act against your irrational beliefs and start working on a task that you have been putting off, then for a time your disturbed feelings will increase, as will your levels of discomfort and the extent of your distorted thoughts. These phenomena will happen because, although you have questioned your irrational beliefs and are rehearsing your new rational beliefs, your brain is still geared up to the effects of your irrational beliefs. Your level of conviction in these irrational beliefs is still stronger at the outset than it is in your rational beliefs. However, if you understand that this increase is part of the process and you accept it as such, then you will persist with the task. As you do so, you will notice that you will increase the impact of your rational beliefs on your feelings, discomfort level and thoughts. So, your feelings will become healthier, the intensity level of your discomfort will come down and your thinking will become more realistic. This process will happen every time you begin a task instead of putting it off, until you have begun to internalize your new rational beliefs and the healthy impact of these beliefs will be experienced more quickly.

Identify and respond to your rationalizations and pseudo-work activities

In this section, I will show you how to deal with the major ways in which you try to deceive yourself that you are not procrastinating, when, in all honesty, you are.

As I discussed in Chapter 5, one of the biggest obstacles you will encounter as you work towards coming out of and staying out of your SDCZ is that you will use one or more rationalizations where you justify to yourself and to others why you have not begun a task that it is in your interests to have started.

As I explained in Chapter 5, it is important that you are honest with yourself and admit that you are using rationalizations to justify what is, in fact, procrastination. When you do this you can identify and respond to the irrational beliefs that really explain why you did not do the task that you agreed to do at a time when you agreed to do it.

As when dealing with your rationalizations, you also need to identify and respond to pseudo-work activities, which you consider to be part of the task but which are really diversionary activities. I discussed these at the beginning of this chapter (see p. 75).

Again, you need to be honest with yourself that these activities are really what I have termed 'pseudo-work' rather than part of the task itself. Then, as with rationalizations, you need to identify and deal with the irrational beliefs that really account for your procrastination.

Use the principle of contingency contracting

Where people who procrastinate go wrong is that they frequently put the pleasant cart before the unpleasant horse, rather than the other way round. Thus, if you truly want to deal effectively with your procrastination problem, it is important for you to postpone engaging with pleasurable activities until you have done the relevant task. This is the principle known as contingency contracting. Thus, you may need to work on a report one evening and there may be a film on the television that same evening that you really want to see. If you tend to procrastinate, you will watch the film and promise yourself that you will work on the report when the film is finished, even though it would be quite late. Instead, why not tape the film and only watch it when you have finished the report or a significant part of it? In this way you will develop good self-discipline skills that will help you stay out of your procrastination-based SDCZ.

Getting out of a rut

When you are in a rut, you know what to do and you know that you can do it. You also know what is going to happen so that there are no surprises in your life. This may well suit some people, and if so, they are not in a self-defeating comfort zone because they don't wish to change. However, you may yearn for a challenge but be reluctant to take a risk. You may move towards taking a risk, but at some point you go back to your SDCZ whenever you become too uncomfortable.

If this applies to you, how can you come out of your rut? By taking the following steps.

Admit that you are in a rut

You won't come out of a rut if you don't think that you are in one. One good way of telling whether or not you are in a rut is to ask yourself the following question: 'If I had a magic wand and I could use it to change my life, but in a realistic way, what would my life be like?' Then reflect on the discrepancy between your life as it is now and your life as you would realistically wish it to be.

If it is realistic for you to work to make the change and you are reluctant to do so because it would mean giving up your sense of familiarity, then you are probably in a rut. Also, if you are dissatisfied with the status quo and you have a sense of being unfulfilled then you are definitely in a rut.

Be clear about your goal

If you have decided that you are in a rut, be clear with yourself concerning what you would like to achieve if you could come out of this rut. Make your goal as specific as you can. The clearer your goal, the more you will be inspired by it.

Recognize that anxiety is what keeps you in your rut

As with other problems where you seek to maintain comfort when it is not healthy for you to do so, you are experiencing an approach–avoidance conflict. You know in your head that you would like do something more challenging with your life, for example, and you approach doing so intellectually. However, when you contemplate actually doing something about changing your life in this respect, you back away from taking action. Your avoidance is motivated by a feeling of anxiety that you would experience if you began to come out of your rut. By staying in your rut, you avoid experiencing anxiety.

Identify what you are most anxious about

As I explained in Chapter 3, a good way of dealing with your SDCZ is to imagine that you have come out of it so you can better assess the factors that keep you in it. So, imagine that you have decided to take steps to come out of your rut and that you have begun to feel anxious. Now ask yourself the following question: 'What am I most anxious about with respect to going for a more challenging life?' If you don't know the answer to this question, use the magic question: 'What one thing would I need when I went for a more challenging life that would eliminate or significantly reduce my anxiety?' The opposite of your answer is what you are most anxious about. Here are some of the most common adversities that people are anxious about concerning coming out of their rut and seeking a more fulfilling life:

- losing a sense of familiarity;
- not knowing what will happen;
- failing to achieve the kind of life you want;
- ending up in no man's land;
- being uncomfortable.

Identify the irrational beliefs that explain why you stay in your rut and the rational alternatives to these irrational beliefs

You will now be familiar with the idea that adversities on their own do not determine our emotions and behaviour. Rather, it is the beliefs that we hold about these adversities that are primarily responsible for how we feel and what we do. Thus, you are anxious about going for a more fulfilling life and choose to stay in your rut, not because of the adversities that you predict will happen if you come out of your SDCZ, but because of the irrational beliefs that you hold about these adversities. Here are some common irrational rigid and extreme beliefs that people hold about the adversities that led them to stay in their rut:

- 'I must not experience a sense of unfamiliarity and it would be awful if I did.'
- 'I must know what will happen if I take a risk and go for what I want. I would not be able to stand such uncertainty.'
- 'I must achieve the kind of life I want if I take a risk. If I don't, I would be a failure.'
- 'I must not end up in no man's land. It would be the end of the world if I do.'
- 'I must be comfortable going for what I want. If I'm not, I would not be able to tolerate it.'

You also need to identify the rational alternatives to your irrational beliefs and see the connection between these and the goals you set with respect to coming out of your rut. Here are the rational alternatives to the irrational beliefs that I presented above.

- 'I would prefer not to experience a sense of unfamiliarity, but that does not mean that I must not do so. If I do, it would be unfortunate but not awful.'
- 'I would like to know what will happen if I take a risk and go for what I want, but I don't have to do so. Tolerating such uncertainty would be a struggle, but I could stand it and it would be worth it to me to do so.'
- 'I would very much like to achieve the kind of life I want if I take a risk, but sadly it's not certain I will succeed. If I don't, I would not be a failure but a fallible human being who has failed on this occasion.'
- 'I don't want to end up in no man's land, but that does not mean that it must not happen. If it does, it would be unfortunate but not the end of the world.'
- 'I want to be comfortable going for what I want, but this is not necessary. If I'm not, it would be hard but I could tolerate it and it would be in my interests to do so.'

Question your beliefs and commit yourself to those that will help you to achieve your goals

The next step is for you to question your irrational beliefs and their rational belief alternatives in order to understand why your irrational beliefs are irrational and why your rational beliefs are rational, and to decide which set of beliefs you wish to commit yourself to acting on in order to achieve your goals. In Appendices 1–4 I outline, in general, the arguments you can use to question (a) your rigid and flexible beliefs; (b) your awfulizing and non-awfulizing beliefs; (c) your discomfort intolerance and tolerance beliefs and (d) your depreciation and acceptance beliefs. Consult these appendices and tailor your arguments to the rigid and extreme beliefs that explain why you stay in your rut and the flexible and non-extreme beliefs that underpin you working to achieve your goals. Make your arguments as persuasive as possible.

Take action while rehearsing your rational beliefs

The purpose of questioning your beliefs is to help you to understand why you should commit yourself to strengthening your conviction in your rational beliefs and to weakening your conviction in your irrational beliefs. In order to strengthen and weaken these respective convictions you need to take action. This action needs to be in line with your rational beliefs and you should aim to take consistent action over time. As you do so, rehearse your rational beliefs before, during and, if necessary, after taking action.

Understand and accept initial increases in disturbed functioning

It is important to understand that when you decide to take action in line with your rational beliefs, while rehearsing them you will still, for a while, experience feelings of anxiety, heightened discomfort and distorted thoughts that stem from the irrational beliefs that are still more persuasive to you than the rational beliefs you are trying to strengthen. This phenomenon is a natural part of the change process and your task is to accept the existence of these disturbed phenomena and resist the urge to go back to your comfortable rut. Instead, continue rehearsing your rational beliefs and acting in line with them. If you do this over time, you will strengthen your conviction in your rational beliefs and they will have a more immediate and beneficial effect on you. Thus, you will feel healthy concern rather than unhealthy anxiety, your discomfort levels will drop and your thinking will be more realistic and balanced. You will also come to see that you were overestimating the negativity of the adversities that you predicted you would face if you came out of your rut (if indeed you encountered them at all) or, if they were in fact as bad as you thought, that you can deal with them healthily.

Identify and respond to your rationalizations and pseudo-work activities

Because your rut is comfortable, you are reluctant to leave it. Therefore you need to find ways of excusing your inaction, both to yourself and to others. Thus, you may use rationalizations to justify why you have chosen to remain in your familiar and comfortable zone or you may try to persuade yourself that the behaviour in which you are engaging is really part of the process of coming out of your rut when it is not.

As I have already stressed, it is important for you to be honest with yourself and admit that you are justifying your inaction with a rationalization or that your action is really pseudo-work.

You can distinguish between a rationalization and a good reason in that, with the former, a jury would say that you could have taken the relevant action, whereas they would say that the latter explains that it was healthy for you not to do so (e.g. you were too ill).

You can tell whether the action you are taking is genuine movement out of your rut towards your goals as opposed to pseudo-work in that when it is the former you are very uncomfortable and with the latter you are not.

Once you have admitted that you are still in your rut and that your rationalizations and/or pseudo-work are just that, then you need to go back and deal with the irrational beliefs that explain why you are not coming out of your rut.

Use the principle of contingency contracting

Unfortunately, coming out of your rut is not a one-off event. It is not as if 'with one bound, you are free'. Rather, it involves you taking a number of steps over time. It would be easy for you to postpone taking these steps until you have done something more enjoyable, but if you do so then you will soon find that you have forgotten about the uncomfortable steps that need to be taken to come out of your rut.

To counter this, resolve to act on the principle of contingency contracting. This principle states that you are more likely to achieve your goals if you postpone pleasure until you have taken the uncomfortable steps that you need to take. This principle is based on the implementation of two aphorisms: 'Discomfort before pleasure' and 'Act when uncomfortable'. People stay in their comfortable but self-defeating ruts because they implement two very different aphorisms: 'Pleasure before discomfort' and 'Act when comfortable'.

Becoming more persistent

Once you have come out of your self-defeating comfort zone you still have the task of staying out of it. This involves you being persistent in doing uncomfortable things in order to achieve your goals. Actually, this is not as daunting as it sounds since it means that you need to repeat what you have done to come out of your SDCZ in the first place.

Once you have viewed your strategy within this context, the question is what would stop you from doing this. Here are two common obstacles to persistence and how to deal with them. I also suggest that you identify and deal with your own obstacles in this area.

Rigid ideas about progress

If you hold a rigid idea about making progress on coming out and staying out of your SDCZ (e.g. 'Once I make progress, I must always maintain it'), then if you have failed to come out of your SDCZ on one occasion you will tend to give up.

In order to deal with this obstacle, you first need to develop a flexible belief about progress (e.g. 'Once I make progress, I would like to always maintain it, but this is not necessary'). Then you need to recognize that backsliding is very common, and when you fail to persist at coming and staying out of your SDCZ, you need (a) to accept yourself for backsliding; (b) to understand why you failed to persist; and (c) to implement your learning on future occasions.

Self-pity about persistence

As you have probably realized by now, coming out and staying out of your SDCZ is hard work and staying out of this zone is probably harder than coming out of it in the first place. If you accept but do not like this reality, then you will be more likely to develop persistence than if you don't accept it. One of the reasons you may not accept it is if you hold a self-pity based irrational belief. If you hold such a belief, you tend to think that because you have worked hard to come out of your SDCZ and are working hard to stay out of it, you deserve a break and that things must be easier than they are. If they are not, you feel sorry for yourself and will seek comfort, and thus you are at risk of backsliding and going back to your SDCZ.

To question this self-pity based irrational belief you need to show yourself that while you might deserve things to be easier for you after all the effort you have made, sadly you don't have to get what you deserve; you are not a poor person, you are a person who is in a poor situation, but one that can be accepted without being liked. If you do develop this non self-pity based rational belief and persist at staying out of your SDCZ even if it is more difficult than you think you deserve, then you will increase your chances of developing persistence and staying out of your self-defeating comfort zone.

In the next chapter, I will show you how you can deal with problems associated with eliminating discomfort.

7

Dealing with problems associated with eliminating discomfort

In this chapter, I will focus on the three main problems that people experience when they try to eliminate discomfort when it is not healthy for them to do so. I will again discuss the main features of these problems and provide general guidance on how to deal with them. As before, I will draw on the material I discussed in Chapters 2–5. More specifically, I will consider the following problems:

- difficulty dealing with urges;
- difficulty tolerating unpleasant feelings and thoughts;
- impatience.

Dealing with urges

If your goal is to abstain from engaging in something that you enjoy but that is not good for you, or to limit your engagement with this activity, then you will soon discover that unless you deal constructively with your urges to engage in the relevant activity, then you won't achieve your goal. Dealing with your urges basically involves not acting on them and realizing that you can tolerate the discomfort of not getting what you want.

In order to deal effectively with your urges, you need to take the following steps.

Recognize the reality of your urge

The reality is that when you are working towards the goal of abstaining from or limiting your engagement with a pleasurable, self-defeating activity, then you will, in all probability, experience an urge to engage in that activity. Some people say when they make a decision to stop smoking they don't feel an urge to smoke, but most people do experience this urge.

Realize that the urge is *not* the problem

Assuming that you will experience an urge to engage with an enjoyable but self-defeating activity, it is important that you recognize that the presence of the urge does not determine whether or not you will act on it. Rather, it is the beliefs that you hold about the urge that are the determining factor here.

Identify your irrational beliefs about your urge and develop rational alternative beliefs

When you habitually act on your urges to engage in a pleasurable but self-defeating activity, you hold a set of irrational beliefs about the urge and the discomfort that you will experience if you don't act on it. These are likely to comprise a rigid belief (e.g. 'I must not experience the urge', 'I must get rid of the urge as quickly as possible' or 'I must have what I want immediately') and a discomfort intolerance belief (e.g. 'I would not be able to tolerate the discomfort if I don't act on my urge and get what I want').

Once you have identified your irrational beliefs you need to develop rational alternatives to them. You will need to have these in place if you are eventually to achieve your goals. As I have already discussed several times in this book, flexible beliefs are rational alternatives to rigid beliefs and discomfort tolerance beliefs are rational alternatives to discomfort intolerance beliefs. Here are the rational alternatives to the irrational beliefs I presented above:

- Flexible belief: 'I would prefer not to experience the urge, but that does not mean that I must not do so'; 'I would like to get rid of the urge as quickly as possible, but I don't have to do so'; or 'I would like to have what I want immediately, but it's not necessary for me to do so.'
- Discomfort tolerance belief: 'It would be hard for me to tolerate the discomfort if I don't act on my urge and get what I want, but I can put up with this discomfort and it would be worth it to me to do so.'

Question your beliefs

As I have mentioned several times in this book, the purpose of questioning your beliefs is (a) to understand why your irrational beliefs are irrational and why your rational beliefs are rational and (b) to commit yourself to strengthening your conviction in the latter and weakening your conviction in the former. I refer you to Appendices 1–4 for guidance about how to question your rational and irrational beliefs. Tailor your arguments to your specific beliefs.

Refrain from acting on your urges and rehearse your rational beliefs

In order to strengthen your conviction in your rational beliefs and to weaken your conviction in your irrational beliefs, you need actual practice at experiencing the urge and not acting on it while rehearsing the appropriate rational beliefs. The more practice you can get at doing this, the better.

Understand and accept variations in the intensity of your urges

Initially, when you don't act on your urge it is important you understand that it will initially increase in intensity even when you rehearse your rational beliefs. If you don't appreciate this fact then you may well act on your urge because you conclude, wrongly, that it will keep on increasing in intensity. The fact is that if you keep refraining from acting on your urge while rehearsing your rational beliefs, the intensity of your urge will decrease and fade, especially if you engage in activity that you would do if you did not experience the urge. However, don't take my word for it: you need to experience these variations in urge intensity to believe it.

Understand and accept the presence of distorted thoughts

It is also important that you understand you will experience distorted thoughts if you don't act on your urges even when you are rehearsing your rational beliefs. Examples of such thoughts might be: 'I will go crazy if I don't have that cigarette'; 'If I don't have that piece of cake now, I will be obsessed with it.' Here is how I suggest that you deal with such distorted thoughts:

1 Acknowledge the existence of such thoughts and understand that they will be in your mind for a while.

2 Understand that the thoughts are products of irrational beliefs which are still active to some degree even though you are rehearsing your rational beliefs. In all probability, they are not realistic premonitions of what will happen if you don't act on your urge.

3 Respond to such thoughts by developing more balanced alternatives to them, but do so only once or twice. Your goal here is to get practice at responding to distorted thoughts and not eliminating them.

4 Get on with whatever you are doing with these thoughts in your mind without re-engaging with them or trying to ignore them. In a phrase, 'Let them be.'

If you follow this sequence you will notice after a while that these thoughts will not be in your mind any more. Take these steps every time distorted thoughts are a problem for you after you act against your urge.

Total abstinence or planned engagement?

Have you made a decision to adopt a total abstinence or a planned engagement regime? Total abstinence involves you not engaging with the pleasurable but self-defeating activity at all. For example, Fay decided to give up smoking altogether. Planned engagement means that you plan to engage with the relevant activity, but you limit your engagement with it (e.g. having two squares of chocolate three times a week rather than a bar a day).

Planned engagement is based on the idea: 'a little of what you fancy does you good'. The problem with this approach is that once you have a taste for the activity, your urge to continue with it is stronger than it would be if you had not engaged with it at all. Thus, if your planned engagement is to have two squares of chocolate, your urge to have more chocolate at that time may well be stronger than it would be if you have no chocolate at all. If you understand that this may well be the case, you will be prepared for it, and if you forcefully rehearse your rational belief about your strengthened urge and are resolved not to act on it, you should be OK.

Expose yourself to your urges, but do so sensibly

When you plan to work towards your goals with respect to abstaining from or limiting your engagement with a pleasurable but self-defeating activity, it is important to think about exposing yourself to your urges as sensibly as you can. This may not be feasible. Thus, if you have decided to give up smoking, you may try to avoid other smokers, but this may not be possible and you may see an advertisement, for example, where someone is smoking which you did not anticipate and which provokes your urge.

However, if you do have control over situations which may provoke your urges, then use the 'challenging, but not overwhelming' principle when exposing yourself to your urges and rehearsing your rational beliefs. This principle states that you can get most out of a self-change programme if you face situations which are challenging for you to deal with rather than those which are overwhelming for you at that time. On the other hand, there is little to be gained from dealing with situations that provide no challenge at all unless you are at the very beginning of such a self-help programme.

Identify and respond to your rationalizations

In dealing with your urges, it is important that you recognize that you may come up with all kinds of rationalizations that seek to justify your engagement with the pleasurable but self-defeating activity. Unless you are honest with yourself about such rationalizations and realize that they are justifications for your engagement with your SDCZ-related behaviour and not true reasons, then you will not reach your goals. Once you are honest with yourself, I suggest that you re-read the material I presented in Chapter 5 on how to deal with rationalizations (see pp. 67–9) and apply the principles that I presented there.

Tolerating unpleasant feelings and thoughts

As human beings, we have an ability that other organisms do not have. We have the ability to react to our own feelings and thoughts. When these feelings and thoughts are unpleasant to us we have a choice. We can examine them and find out what they are about and take appropriate action or we can try to get rid of them as quickly as possible. When we do the latter we make ourselves comfortable in the short term, but we don't learn from our feelings and/ or thoughts and we may well unwittingly perpetuate them by not dealing with them.

So if you tend to get rid of negative feelings and thoughts, what can you do to examine them instead? In order to examine them you need to be able to tolerate them long enough to do just that. I suggest that you take the following steps.

Identify the unpleasant feeling or thought that you would like to examine

In order to deal with your unpleasant feeling or thought you need to identify it. This, of course, may be difficult because you have probably become adept at avoiding or eliminating it. However, you probably have some idea of what feeling or thought you are avoiding. If so, make a note of it.

Recognize that it is your irrational beliefs about this feeling/ thought that lead you to want to avoid or eliminate it

The 'ABC' model of RECBT clearly states that you seek to avoid or eliminate an unpleasant feeling or thought because of the irrational beliefs that you hold about it.

If your feelings and thoughts are a threat to your self-esteem, your irrational beliefs are as follows:

> *Rigid belief (e.g. 'I must not think of harming my child')*
> *Self-depreciation belief (e.g. 'If I think of harming my child, there is something wrong with me').*

If you find the experience of your unpleasant feeling or thought intolerable (without it being a threat to your self-esteem) then your irrational beliefs are as follows:

> *Rigid belief (e.g. 'I must not experience anxiety')*
> *Discomfort intolerance belief (e.g. 'If I experience anxiety, I will not be able to tolerate it').*

Identify rational alternatives to these beliefs

In order to examine your unpleasant feelings or thoughts you need to hold a set of rational beliefs about them so that you can do so. Here are the rational alternatives to the irrational beliefs presented above.

To deal with unpleasant feelings or thoughts which do involve a self-esteem threat, your rational beliefs are as follows:

Flexible belief (e.g. 'I really don't like thinking of harming my child, but that does not mean that I must not do so')

Self-acceptance belief (e.g. 'If I think of harming my child, there may be something wrong, but not with me as a whole person. I am a fallible human who has unwanted thoughts that need to be examined').

To examine your unpleasant feelings or thoughts that do not involve a threat to your self-esteem, your rational beliefs are as follows:

Flexible belief (e.g. 'I don't want to experience anxiety, but that does not mean that I must not do so')

Discomfort tolerance belief (e.g. 'If I experience anxiety, it's hard to tolerate, but I can do so and it would be worth it to me to do so').

Question these beliefs

Again, the purpose of questioning your beliefs is (a) to understand why your irrational beliefs are irrational and why your rational beliefs are rational, and (b) to commit yourself to strengthening your conviction in the latter and weakening your conviction in the former. I refer you to Appendices 1–4 for guidance about how to question your rational and irrational beliefs. Tailor your arguments to your specific beliefs.

Rehearse your rational beliefs, but recognize that when you focus on your unpleasant feelings/thoughts initially they may increase in intensity

In order to examine your unpleasant feelings or thoughts you need to rehearse your rational beliefs as you face them. However, when you do so, understand that your feelings or thoughts may initially increase in intensity, since your irrational beliefs are to some extent still active even though you are rehearsing their rational alternatives. If you accept this and get on with the business of examining them, they will reduce in intensity.

Use the 'ABC' framework to deal with your unpleasant feelings and thoughts

The best way of examining your unpleasant feelings and thoughts is to regard them as emotional and thinking consequences ('C') of beliefs ('B') about some adversity ('A'). In doing so, I suggest that you use RECBT's 'ABC' framework that I outlined in Chapters 2 and 3.

Developing patience

If you tend to be impatient, it is likely that you avoid situations in which you may have to wait, for example. If you can't avoid such situations, you may experience unhealthy anger and make impulsive and rash decisions. While it is clear why avoiding negative situations where you have to wait is a comfort zone, you may well ask why anger and impulsiveness should be a comfort zone, albeit a self-defeating one for you, since it doesn't seem to be that comfortable. The answer is that it helps you escape or deal with something that you deem much worse – waiting.

In order to develop patience about waiting and about other situations in which you display impatience, you need to take the following steps:

Acknowledge that you are impatient and that it is a problem for you

As with other 'problems', unless you acknowledge that you are impatient you are not likely to target it for change. Even if you do recognize that you are impatient, you may not acknowledge that it is a problem for you.

Are you impatient?

Unless you are practised at self-deception, if you experience impatience you are likely to own up to this. I do not mean to imply that if you are impatient then you are this way across the board – far from it. Indeed, I would say that most people who experience impatience in certain areas of their lives may well display a good deal of patience in other areas.

Is your impatience a problem for you?

Once you have identified areas of your life in which you experience impatience, you are ready to consider whether it is problematic for you or not. To consider this question fully you need to do the following:

- Develop an alternative to impatience that may be healthier for you.
- Write down the short-term advantages of both responses to you and to others.
- Write down the short-term disadvantages of both responses to you and to others.
- Write down the long-term advantages of both responses to you and to others.
- Write down the long-term disadvantages of both responses to you and to others.
- Reflect on your responses and decide whether on balance your impatience is a problem for you. If so, proceed to the next step.

In considering these points, you may find it helpful to copy out the form provided in Figure 1 (see page 98) and complete it for yourself.

Set clear goals

While you were considering whether or not your impatience is a problem for you, I suggested that you think of a potentially helpful alternative. Now that you have decided that your impatience is a problem for you, I suggest that you make your goals with respect to this problem clearer, so that you know what you are aiming for. Specify the situations in which you are impatient and compare your impatient response with a more patient response. If you were patient in your listed situations, how would your feelings, thinking and behaviour be different? Be realistic here rather than idealistic. I suggest that you consider the case of Harry (see Chapter 2) if you need some help in doing this.

Impatience

Advantages of impatience

Short-term advantages

For myself:
1 ....
2 ....
3 ....
4 ....
5 ....

For others:
1 ....
2 ....
3 ....
4 ....
5 ....

Long-term advantages

For myself:
1 ....
2 ....
3 ....
4 ....
5 ....

For others:
1 ....
2 ....
3 ....
4 ....
5 ....

Disadvantages of impatience

Short-term disadvantages

For myself:
1 ....
2 ....
3 ....
4 ....
5 ....

For others:
1 ....
2 ....
3 ....
4 ....
5 ....

Long-term disadvantages

For myself:
1 ....
2 ....
3 ....
4 ....
5 ....

For others:
1 ....
2 ....
3 ....
4 ....
5 ....

Figure 1 A cost-benefit analysis of patience and impatience

Patience

Advantages of patience

Short-term advantages

For myself:

1 ....

2 ....

3 ....

4 ....

5 ....

For others:

1 ....

2 ....

3 ....

4 ....

5 ....

Long-term advantages

For myself:

1 ....

2 ....

3 ....

4 ....

5 ....

For others:

1 ....

2 ....

3 ....

4 ....

5 ....

Disadvantages of patience

Short-term disadvantages

For myself:

1 ....

2 ....

3 ....

4 ....

5 ....

For others:

1 ....

2 ....

3 ....

4 ....

5 ....

Long-term disadvantages

For myself:

1 ....

2 ....

3 ....

4 ....

5 ....

For others:

1 ....

2 ....

3 ....

4 ....

5 ....

Realize that beliefs largely determine whether you are impatient or patient

It is important that you realize that the situations you outlined in which you are impatient do not on their own determine this response. Rather, it is the beliefs that you hold about these situations that largely determine whether your response is marked by impatience or by patience.

Identify the irrational beliefs that underpin your impatience and develop rational alternatives that will underpin your patience

RECBT's approach to understanding why people stay in or keep out of self-defeating comfort zones is based on the idea that when you go to your SDCZ (or stay in it) the beliefs that you hold about salient features of the situation you are in are irrational, and when you come out of or stay out of this same zone these beliefs are rational.

Thus, your task here is to identify the irrational beliefs that underpin your impatient response in the situations in which you experience and/or display impatience. The following are common irrational (i.e. rigid and extreme) beliefs that underpin impatience.

- 'I have to have what I want quickly and I can't bear to wait to get it.'
- 'I absolutely should not have to wait for things, and others and/or the world are rotten for expecting me to wait.'
- 'Others must do tasks quickly and efficiently and if they don't I can't bear it.'

The rational alternatives to these beliefs that underpin patience are as follows:

- 'I would like to have what I want quickly, but my preference does not have to be met. I can bear to wait to get it, even though it's difficult, and it is worth it to me to do so.'
- 'I would prefer not to have to wait for things, but it does not have to be that way. Others and/or the world are certainly not rotten for expecting me to wait. They are fallible, and while it's bad that they don't prioritize me, they really don't have to do so.'

- 'It would be nice if others did tasks quickly and efficiently, but they don't have to do so. It's hard for me to put up with it when they don't, but I can bear it, and it's worth bearing.'

Question your beliefs

As I have stated several times before in this book, the purpose of questioning your beliefs is (a) to understand why your irrational beliefs are irrational and why your rational beliefs are rational, and (b) to commit yourself to strengthening your conviction in the latter and weakening your conviction in the former. I refer you to Appendices 1–4 for guidance about how to question your rational and irrational beliefs. Tailor your arguments to your specific beliefs.

Apply your rational beliefs in relevant situations

Now that you have understood why your rational beliefs are rational and your irrational beliefs are irrational it is time to apply this knowledge in actual situations by rehearsing your rational beliefs in situations to which you have previously responded with impatience. Use the 'challenging, but not overwhelming' principle while doing so. This involves you facing situations that moderately test your patience rather than those that pose too much of a challenge. There is little to gain facing situations that you already can deal with patiently.

While facing such a situation, I suggest that you rehearse your rational beliefs both before facing the situation and as you face it. Really try to believe what you are rehearsing and act in ways that are consistent with it. Afterwards, review your experience and identify and learn from any difficulties that you encounter (see Chapter 5).

Understand and accept that your level of discomfort and your distorted thoughts will increase temporarily

When you respond impatiently to situations that involve you putting up with things you find difficult, you are trying to eliminate discomfort. Thus, when you stay in such situations your level of discomfort will rise temporarily despite you rehearsing your rational beliefs. This is because your irrational beliefs are still active and you are remaining in the situation you would previously have left.

However, if you persist with your rational rehearsal and remain in the situation, your level of discomfort will come down.

This is also the case with the thinking that you are aware of if you stay and rehearse rational beliefs. This thinking will be quite distorted since your irrational beliefs are still active, but if you understand it and let such thinking be without engaging with it (aside from briefly responding to it once you notice it) and without trying to eliminate it, you will eventually discover that such thinking has faded away.

Utilize your time more productively while you wait

Once you have gained practice at tolerating aversive situations and responding to them with patience, you can then find ways of spending your time productively while you wait. For example, Harry spent his time while waiting in supermarket queues responding to emails on his phone or doing Sudoku puzzles. Instead of getting angry at others' inefficiency, you can show them ways of working more efficiently if they are so interested. However, don't employ these methods to use time more productively before working to strengthen your conviction in your rational beliefs. If you do so, your impatience will soon overwhelm these practical techniques.

Give yourself more time than you need

I once saw a man for counselling who had a dreadful problem with impatience. He decided that if everything was in his favour, then it should take him 30 minutes to get from his office to the railway station to catch his train. Unfortunately, matters were rarely in his favour and, rather than modify his schedule to accommodate the world (which would have involved him giving himself more time to catch his train), he tried to modify the world to accommodate his schedule. Thus, he would push people out of his way, rant loudly against the inefficient tube system and run at top speed even though he was overweight and it was dangerous for him to do so. Needless to say, the world did not change, but his problems deepened.

As part of an overall approach to developing greater patience (but after you have gained experience at rehearsing your rational beliefs while facing situations that you see as 'trying your patience'), I do suggest that you give yourself more time than a task would take.

This will help you to deal with things going wrong with greater equanimity. Whenever I am in writing mode, for example, I estimate how long a book will take me to write and then I add 50 per cent to this schedule. I do this to help myself deal with interruptions to my writing schedule that life inevitably throws up. Using this approach, I usually meet my schedule with time to spare. Yes, I could practise patience in dealing with interruptions to the schedule without the added 50 per cent, but I want to be the master of my schedule rather than allowing the world to dictate it. Being more generous with your 'time–task' allocation will help you develop greater patience when the going gets tough, but only if you are also working to adopt a rational philosophy that will help you respond with greater patience to life's difficulties.

In the final chapter, I provide some advice about how to get the most out of this book.

8

Self-help books and comfort zones

I have written almost 30 self-help books over my career. I have done so because I genuinely believe that people can derive a lot of benefit from applying the wisdom and techniques of Rational-Emotive Cognitive Behavioural Therapy (RECBT).

However, I also know three things about self-help books that apply to the entire genre and not just to the books that I and my RECBT colleagues have written.

The first thing that I know about self-help books is that most people who buy them don't read them. They put them on their shelf and appear to act on the notion (which they would never admit to consciously) that somehow the knowledge contained in those unread pages will make a difference to their lives. If only it could!

The second thing I know about self-help books is that most people who read them don't apply them. These people think that reading is sufficient to make a difference in their lives. Sadly, it rarely will. Reading will give you knowledge, but it will not provide you with the experience of applying that knowledge. It is this application that is necessary for you to benefit from a self-help book such as this one. Would you expect to learn to swim from reading a book about it but without getting into the water and trying out the strokes? Of course you wouldn't. So why would you expect that reading a self-help book without applying its teachings will be any different?

The third thing that I know about self-help books is that of the people who will apply what they read, most won't maintain their application. They won't keep going. In particular, they give up when the going gets tough. Or maybe a new self-help book comes out that promises gains without effort. No, to really get the most out of any self-help book you need to apply its teachings consistently over time and anticipate and learn from the obstacles that you will experience along the way.

In summary, remember four things:

1 When you buy this book but don't read it, you are entering a self-defeating comfort zone where you think that having the book will magically make a difference to you.

2 If you read this book but don't apply its teachings, you are entering a self-defeating comfort zone where you think that reading the book will magically make a difference to you.

3 If you apply what I have to say in this book but do so infrequently and without consistency or you give up when the going gets tough, you are entering a self-defeating comfort zone where you think that a little obstacle-free effort will magically make a difference to you.

4 However, if you read, apply and keep applying the teachings found in this book, and if you anticipate and deal with obstacles to change head on, then you will come out of these magical self-defeating comfort zones and stay out of them. In doing so you will, in all probability, live a more fulfilling life. Are you prepared to do this?

Appendix 1

Reasons why rigid beliefs are false, illogical and have largely
unhealthy consequences and flexible beliefs are true, logical
and have largely healthy consequences

Rigid belief

A rigid belief is false

For such a demand to be true the
demanded conditions would already
have to exist when they do not. Or as
soon as you make a demand then these
demanded conditions would have to
come into existence. Both positions are
clearly false or inconsistent with reality.

A rigid belief is illogical

A rigid belief is based on the same desire
as a flexible belief but is transformed as
follows:

*'I prefer that "x" happens (or does not
happen) . . . and therefore this absolutely
must (or must not) happen.'*

The first ('I prefer that "x" happens [or
does not happen]') is not rigid, but the
second ('and therefore this must [or
must not] happen') is rigid. As such, a
rigid belief is illogical since one cannot
logically derive something rigid from
something that is not rigid.

A rigid belief has largely unhealthy consequences

A rigid belief has largely unhealthy
consequences because it tends to lead
to unhealthy negative emotions,
unconstructive behaviour and highly
distorted and biased subsequent
thinking when the person is facing an
adversity.

Flexible belief

A flexible belief is true

A flexible belief is true because its two
component parts are true. You can
prove that you have a particular desire
and can provide reasons why you want
what you want. You can also prove
that you do not have to get what you
desire.

A flexible belief is logical

A flexible belief is logical since both
parts are not rigid and thus the second
component logically follows from the
first. Thus, consider the following
flexible belief:

*'I prefer that "x" happens (or does not
happen) . . . but this does not mean that
it must (or must not) happen.'*

The first component ('I prefer that "x"
happens [or does not happen]') is not
rigid and the second ('but this does
not mean that it must [or must not]
happen') is also non-rigid. Thus, a
flexible belief is logical because it
comprises two non-rigid parts
connected together logically.

A flexible belief has largely healthy consequences

A flexible belief has largely healthy
consequences because it tends to
lead to healthy negative emotions,
constructive behaviour and realistic
and balanced subsequent thinking
when the person is facing an adversity.

Appendix 2

Reasons why awfulizing beliefs are false, illogical and have largely unhealthy consequences and non-awfulizing beliefs are true, logical and have largely healthy consequences

Awfulizing belief

An awfulizing belief is false

When you hold an awfulizing belief about your 'A', this belief is based on the following ideas:

1. Nothing could be worse.
2. The event in question is worse than 100 per cent bad.
3. No good could possibly come from this bad event.

All three ideas are patently false and thus your awfulizing belief is false.

An awfulizing belief is illogical

An awfulizing belief is based on the same evaluation of badness as a non-awfulizing belief, but is transformed as follows:

'It is bad if "x" happens (or does not happen) . . . and therefore it is awful if it does happen (or does not happen).'

The first component ('It is bad if "x" happens [or does not happen]') is non-extreme, but the second ('and therefore it is awful if it does [or does not] happen') is extreme. As such, an awfulizing belief is illogical since one cannot logically derive something extreme from something that is non-extreme.

An awfulizing belief has largely unhealthy consequences

An awfulizing belief has largely unhealthy consequences because it tends to lead to unhealthy negative emotions, unconstructive behaviour and highly distorted and biased subsequent thinking when the person is facing an adversity.

Non-awfulizing belief

A non-awfulizing belief is true

When you hold a non-awfulizing belief about your 'A', this belief is based on the following ideas:

1. Things could always be worse.
2. The event in question is less than 100 per cent bad.
3. Good could come from this bad event.

All three ideas are clearly true and thus your non-awfulizing belief is true.

A non-awfulizing belief is logical

A non-awfulizing belief is logical since both parts are non-rigid and thus the second component logically follows from the first. Consider the following non-awfulizing belief:

'It is bad if "x" happens (or does not happen) . . . but it is not awful if "x" happens (or does not happen).'

The first component ('It is bad if "x" happens [or does not happen]') is non-extreme and the second ('but it is not awful if it does [or does not] happen') is also non-extreme. Thus, a non-awfulizing belief is logical because it comprises two non-extreme parts connected together logically.

A non-awfulizing belief has largely healthy consequences

A non-awfulizing belief has largely healthy consequences because it tends to lead to healthy negative emotions, constructive behaviour and realistic and balanced subsequent thinking when the person is facing an adversity.

Appendix 3

Reasons why discomfort intolerance beliefs are false,
illogical and have largely unhealthy consequences
and why discomfort tolerance beliefs are true, logical
and have largely healthy consequences

Discomfort intolerance belief

A discomfort intolerance belief is false

When you hold a discomfort intolerance belief about your 'A', this belief is based on the following ideas, which are all false:

1 I will die or disintegrate if the discomfort continues to exist.
2 I will lose the capacity to experience happiness if the discomfort continues to exist.
3 Even if I could tolerate it, the discomfort is not worth tolerating.

All three ideas are patently false and thus your discomfort intolerance belief is false.

A discomfort intolerance belief is illogical

A discomfort intolerance belief is based on the same sense of struggle as a discomfort tolerance belief, but is transformed as follows:

'It would be difficult for me to tolerate it if "x" happens (or does not happen) . . . and therefore it would be intolerable.'

The first component ('It would be difficult for me to tolerate it if "x" happens [or does not happen]') is non-extreme, but the second ('and therefore it would be intolerable') is extreme. As such, a discomfort intolerance belief is illogical since one cannot logically derive something extreme from something that is non-extreme.

Discomfort tolerance belief

A discomfort tolerance belief is true

When you hold a discomfort tolerance belief about your 'A', this belief is based on the following ideas, which are all true:

1 I will struggle if the discomfort continues to exist, but I will neither die nor disintegrate.
2 I will not lose the capacity to experience happiness if the discomfort continues to exist, although this capacity will be temporarily diminished.
3 The discomfort is worth tolerating.

All three ideas are patently true and thus your discomfort tolerance belief is true.

A discomfort tolerance belief is logical

A discomfort tolerance belief is logical since both parts are non-extreme and thus the second component logically follows from the first. Thus, consider following discomfort tolerance belief:

'It would be difficult for me to tolerate it if "x" happens (or does not happen) . . . but it would not be intolerable (and it would be worth tolerating).'

The first component ('It would be difficult for me to tolerate it if "x" happens [or does not happen]') is non-extreme and the second ('but it would not be intolerable [and it would be worth tolerating]') is also non-extreme. Thus, a discomfort tolerance belief is logical because it comprises two non-extreme parts connected together logically.

A discomfort intolerance belief has largely unhealthy consequences

A discomfort intolerance belief has largely unhealthy consequences because it tends to lead to unhealthy negative emotions, unconstructive behaviour and highly distorted and biased subsequent thinking when the person is facing an adversity.

A discomfort tolerance belief has largely healthy consequences

A discomfort tolerance belief has largely healthy consequences because it tends to lead to healthy negative emotions, constructive behaviour and realistic and balanced subsequent thinking when the person is facing an adversity.

Appendix 4

Reasons why depreciation beliefs are false, illogical and have largely unhealthy consequences and acceptance beliefs are true, logical and have largely healthy consequences

Depreciation belief

A depreciation belief is false

When you hold a depreciation belief in the face of your 'A', this belief is based on the following ideas, which are all false:

1 A person (self or other) or life can legitimately be given a single global rating that defines his, her or its essence and the worth of a person or of life is dependent upon conditions that change (e.g. my worth goes up when I do well and goes down when I don't do well).
2 A person or life can be rated on the basis of one of his or her or its aspects.

Both of these ideas are patently false and thus your depreciation belief is false.

A depreciation belief is illogical

A depreciation belief is based on the idea that the whole of a person or of life can logically be defined by one of his, her or its parts. Thus:

'"A" is bad . . . and therefore I am bad.'

This is known as the part–whole error, which is illogical.

A depreciation belief has largely unhealthy consequences

A depreciation belief has largely unhealthy consequences because it tends to lead to unhealthy negative emotions, unconstructive behaviour and highly distorted and biased subsequent thinking when the person is facing an adversity.

Acceptance belief

An acceptance belief is true

When you hold an acceptance belief in the face of your 'A', this belief is based on the following ideas, which are all true:

1 A person (self or other) or life cannot legitimately be given a single global rating that defines his, her or its essence and worth, as far as the person or life has it, is not dependent upon conditions that change (e.g. my worth stays the same whether or not I do well).
2 Discrete aspects of a person, and life, can be legitimately rated, but a person or life cannot be legitimately rated on the basis of these discrete aspects.

Both of these ideas are patently true and thus your acceptance belief is true.

An acceptance belief is logical

An acceptance belief is based on the idea that the whole of a person or of life cannot be defined by one or more of his, her or its parts. Thus:

'"A"is bad, but this does not mean that I am bad, I am a fallible human being even though "A" happened.'

Here the part–whole illogical error is avoided. Rather it is held that the whole incorporates the part, which is logical.

An acceptance belief has largely healthy consequences

An acceptance belief has largely healthy consequences because it tends to lead to healthy negative emotions, constructive behaviour and realistic and balanced subsequent thinking when the person is facing an adversity.

Index